SOCIO-POLITICAL THOUGHT IN AFRICAN LITERATURE

16 ⁰⁰ 10/333

Socio-political Thought
in African Literature:

Weusi?

G-C. M. Mutiso

Senior Lecturer in Government
University of Nairobi

Macmillan

First published 1974 by
THE MACMILLAN PRESS LTD
London and Basingstoke
Associated companies in New York
Dublin Melbourne Johannesburg and Madras

SBN 333 15556 4

Photoset and printed
in Great Britain by
REDWOOD BURN LIMITED
Trowbridge & Esher

For Rho and Tola

As I sit here with my mouth closed does not mean that I have not got a strong inside or that what our leader has said does not enter my inside.

Gabriel Okara

Contents

Foreword   *page* ix

Acknowledgements   xiii

Part One: Non-Literary Content in Literature   1

  1   Derivation of Social Theory from Literature   3
  2   The Social and Political Nature of African Writing   9

Part Two: Group and Individual Identity in the African
    Context   15

  3   The Literati   17
  4   The Bureaucrats and Professionals   31
  5   The Politicians and the Political Process   39
  6   The Role of Women   51
  7   The Rural–Urban Contradiction   73
  8   The Individual–Community Contradiction   83

Part Three: African Identity in the World Context   93

  9   Interpretations of the Past, the Present and the
       Future   95
10   Pan-Africanism   117
11   Social Change   123

Notes   133
Select Biographies   143
Bibliography   165
Index   181

Foreword

Literally, *weusi* means blackness. Many in Africa have yearned for a black ideal as the antithesis to colonial bondage. By studying the thought in African literature, we shall document in this book the writers' view of *weusi* and the factors which deny it. The writers pose the question whether what exists is *weusi*, hence the query in our title!

For the purposes of this book literature, by definition, embraces the novels, plays, short stories and poetry written originally in English by indigenous Africans in the countries which were formerly parts of the British Empire in Africa. The period of time covered is that from the end of the Second World War to 1967. The rationale for the selection of this particular period is twofold. Firstly, not much literature was written in Africa before 1945. Secondly, an increase in literary output after the war took place at a time when rapid social and political change in Africa was being crystallised in the crusade against colonialism and the push toward nationhood. The passions aroused at this time found expression in the growing body of creative literary works.

Several qualifications are in order concerning the scope of this book. First, it should be emphasised that what we are concerned with here is literature *per se* – that is, material that inevitably deals with certain aspects of the social situation which the writer deems important but that is not written with the purpose of expounding some specific social or political idea. Excluded, therefore, are the writings of political leaders who write not necessarily in terms of choosing values and projecting these into the society but rather from an involved political point of view. The works of the Nkrumahs, the Nassers, the Kenyattas and the Nyereres may be classified in this unique group. Most of the research in the area of the political and social thought of Africa has dealt with this type of writing.

A second category of material that has been left out is the attempts of scholars to develop distinct political and social theories concerning Africa. Examples of this would be Professor Abraham's *The Mind of Africa*[1] and Chiekh Anta Diop's *The*

Cultural Unity of Negro Africa.[2] Such writings seek to arrive at
social or political theories which are internally consistent and
supposedly relevant to the African situation. The authors
argue strongly for the uniqueness of the African situation but
see the possible applicability to it of political and social ideas
that were essentially developed in the West.

Third, there is a large body of literature in African languages
which has not been included in this study. Some of the literature is available in translation; however, the bulk of it is not.
Since it would have been difficult, if not impossible, to master
all of the languages involved, none of this material has been included. Furthermore, literature which was written down after
1945 but which was previously part of the oral tradition has
been omitted on the basis of two considerations. First, it represents a codification of a past era. Second, it is not clear that the
available 'written' oral tradition literature is representative of
the total amount of such work, most of which has never been
transcribed.

A word should be said, also, concerning the nations covered
by this study. Not all the former British colonies have produced
literature. There has been no literature – according to our
definition – from Swaziland, the Sudan, Somali or Zambia.
The Cameroons has been excluded since its literature is basically French, although Dipoko Mbella Sonne writes both in
English and in French. South African literature has been
excluded on the basis that it is predominantly protest literature, as Lewis Nkosi and Ezekiel Mphahlele point out.[3] Dennis
Brutus, although born in Southern Rhodesia, has until recently
lived in and writes about South Africa. He considers himself a
South African and hence has been excluded.

The countries actually covered include Lesotho, Botswana,
Malawi, Southern Rhodesia, Tanzania, Kenya, Uganda, Nigeria, Ghana, Sierra Leone and Gambia. Nigeria has the greatest
output of literature in this group. This has resulted in a built-in
bias in the present work, since a considerable amount of the
literature it deals with is taken from one country. Some of the
countries included could conceivably have been excluded had a
quantity principle been employed. Botswana and Tanzania,
for example, do not have a major novel to their credit, although
they have smatterings of poems and occasional plays and short

stories in journals. But in the opinion of the author, inclusion by rejection of the quantity principle rather than exclusion by its use was desirable to the extent that a larger sample tended to confirm the hypothesis that all African literature deals with similar major problems regardless of the specific country from which it originates.

These problems are concerned first of all with individual and group identity in society, and second with societal identity in the world context. The distinction between these two ideas provides the basis for the organisation of this book. The first theme, explored in Part Two, takes the form of an examination of the various spokesmen and issues utilised by the writers to expound social and political ideas. The spokesmen are the literati (including the intellectuals), the bureaucrats, the politicians, and emancipated women. The issues include the rural–urban contradiction and its effect on the individual and society, and the individual–community contradiction and its relationship to the issue of social change.

The second theme – societal identity in the world context, the subject of Part Three – will be broken down under three sub-headings. One is the argument for the uniqueness and glory of the African past and culture and the denial of these qualities in the writings of the West. This is a preoccupation of all of the writers studied. Another aspect of the theme, the argument that African identity is ultimately tied to the question of Pan-Africanism in spite of disagreement as to how this goal can be achieved, is prominent in the post-independence period. A third aspect is the writers' perceptions of social change and the groups considered by them to be purveyors of change.

Various problems confront the writer who engages in research in the area of African literature. To the best of this author's knowledge there was previously no complete bibliography on African literature as that term has been defined for the purposes of this book. Compilation of a bibliography was therefore begun by examining Janheinz Jahn's *Bibliography of Neo-African Literature from Africa, America and the Caribbean.*[4] This volume obviously takes in a broader geographical area than the present work as it also includes the Caribbean and Black America. However, it does not distinguish literature from anthropology, history or ethnology, among other fields, so its usefulness was limited.

The bibliography compiled from Jahn was then checked with two other sources, M. Amosu's *A Preliminary Bibliography of Creative African Writing in the European Languages,*[5] and the bibliography in Martin Tucker's *Africa in Modern Literature,*[6] which also includes European writing on Africa. Additional information was gained by referring to the Book Review sections of the following periodicals: *Africa Report, Présence Africaine, Black Orpheus, Nigeria Magazine, Books Abroad, Journal of Modern African Studies* and *Transition.* The resulting augmented bibliography was further extended by checking and adding items found in Judith I. Gleason's bibliography in *This Africa,*[7] and in Barbara Abrash's *Black African Literature in English since 1952.*[8] The latter work was the most complete and up-to-date bibliography available, but there are additional books collected by this author which do not appear in Miss Abrash's work.

One other very important point should be made concerning what this book does and does not attempt to achieve. It was suggested earlier in this chapter that there are three main categories in which the writings of Africans may be classified, namely, political writings, theoretical writings, and literature. To repeat, we deal here only with the last category – that is, an identification of the perceptions of African creative writers – and not with any material that is clearly expository in style or intention. In the final analysis, any attempt to understand African social and political thought has to come to terms with the ideas in all three categories and the problem of integrating them. Only on the basis of such a synthesis of concepts can anything approaching a system of African social and political thought be built. Obviously from this point of view the present undertaking is only a portion of what should be a four-part study culminating in the construction of a general theory of African social and political thought. Perhaps with this first step taken completion of such a work can be anticipated in the not-too-distant future.

Finally, in terms of materials used I have attempted to cover all published work up to 1968. A few very critical books have come out since the completion of this work. These will be covered in a subsequent work showing changing directions especially in eastern Africa's writing.

Acknowledgements

The author and publishers wish to thank the copyright-holders (named in brackets) who have kindly given permission for the use of extracts from the following copyright material:

Chinua Achebe, 'The Black Writer's Burden' (*Présence Africaine*, No. 59 (1956)); Chinua Achebe, *No Longer At Ease* and *A Man of the People* (William Heinemann Ltd); T. M. Aluko, *One Man, One Matchet* (Heinemann Educational Books Ltd); R. E. G. Armattoe, *Deep Down the Black Man's Mind* and Dennis Chikude, *Africa Sings* (Arthur H. Stockwell Ltd); Michael Dei-Anang, *Wayward Lines From Africa* (Lutterworth Press); Obi Egbuna, *Wind Versus Polygamy* (Faber & Faber Ltd); Cyprian Ekwnsi, *Beautiful Feathers* (Hutchinson Publishing Group Ltd); Albert Kayper Mensah, 'The Ghosts' from *A Book of African Verse*, ed. J. Reed and Clive Wake (Heinemann Educational Books Ltd); Simon Kihohia, *There Had Always Been* (East African Publishing House); James Ngugi, *Weep Not, Child* (Heinemann Educational Books Ltd); Abioseh Nicol, 'The Meaning of Africa' from *A Book of African Verse*, ed. J. Reed and Clive Wake (Heinemann Educational Books Ltd); T. C. Nwosu, 'The Unbeliever' (T. C. Nwosu); Onoura Nzekwu, *Highlife for Lizards* (Hutchinson Publishing Group Ltd); Okot p'Bitek, *No Bride Price* (East African Publishing House); John Pepper Clark, 'In the Cult of the Freen' from *Reed in the Tide* (Longman Group Ltd); Lenrie Peters, *Satellites* (Heinemann Educational Books Ltd); David Rubadiri, *Song of Lawind* (East African Publishing House); Raymond Sarif Easmon, *The New Patriots* (Longman Group Ltd); Mabel Segun, 'Second Olympus' from *English*, xv, No. 90 (the English Association); Wole Soyinka, *Kongi's Harvest* (Oxford University Press); Clive H. Wake, 'African Literary Criticism' (*Comparative Literature Studies*, i (1964) 197–8).

The publishers have made every effort to trace the copyright-holders but if they have inadvertently overlooked any, they will be pleased to make the necessary arrangement at the first opportunity.

Part One: Non-literary Content in Literature

1 Derivation of Social Theory from Literature

All literature, to the extent that it deals with individuals in society, contains elements of social and political theory. Obviously the creative writer does not always write with the intention of propagating a particular idea, but he cannot create in a vacuum. When he depicts a character or an incident his judgements come into play, thereby revealing some of the value choices he has made either consciously or unconsciously. All literature depicts the values of the people and the period. This is to say that however imaginative a writer may be, the framework of his writings must always be the society he knows. Even when he transcends his own historical period, he is choosing other periods for comparison with his understanding of the historical present. As Joseph Blotner states in his study *The Political Novel*:

> Not only does the novelist have complete freedom in time and space, he has the right to use any of the devices found attractive in communication since the first articulate primate squatting in the firelight gave his interpretation of experience to his hairy brothers. The point of the story can be driven home or made palatable with laughter, suspense, or a cops-and-robbers chase that will make it memorable.[1]

Derivation of social and political theory from literature does not depend on the question of whether it is written basically as political literature or not, since the artist at all times goes beyond recording society. The artist – the novelist or poet in particular – also plays a crucial role in a society in explaining and interpreting the nuances of that society to those without. Enlightenment concerning the values and activities of a society can thus be facilitated by studying its literature. According to

3

Blotner,

> If most of [a society's] novels deal with underground activities, coups d'etat, or revolutions, [the reader] is justified in assuming that this is a people which takes its politics seriously and emotionally. If most of the novels concern parliamentary give and take, clever use of rules, strategic marches and countermarches, he has a right to conclude that this national group has achieved some degree of political sophistication.[2]

Indeed, some writers have suggested that the reflection of social and political values in a society's literature is often the most accurate index as to what that society is really like. Charles Poore writes that:

> A nation's novelists are usually more effective than its statesmen in telling us about that country's people and their way of living. The reason is plain. The novelist has every advantage. A statesman must deal in policy-riddled national generalities, a novelist can concentrate on individuals, their lives, hates, and hazardous fortunes.[3]

Above all else the artist, as Leo Lowenthal points out, reacts to society.

> Man is born, strives, loves, suffers and dies in any society, but it is the portrayal of how he reacts to these common human experiences that matters, since they almost invariably have a social nexus. Precisely because literature presents the whole man in depth, the artist tends to justify or defy society rather than be its passive chronicler.[4]

Thus the creative person tends to delineate for society what in his view are the most desirable choices among competing values. George Orwell is even more adamant on this point. He categorically states that the artist always has a

> desire to push the world in a certain direction, to alter other people's idea of the type of society that they should strive after . . . no book is genuinely free of political bias. The opinion that art should have nothing to do with politics is itself a political attitude.[5]

In this book we shall examine the social and political perceptions of African creative writers concerning the past, the transitional present and the future of African society. From what they
produce as literature we should be able to extrapolate the major
social and political concepts that will be used for the social-
isation of present and future generations. Largely because of
the nature of the period covered, the writers have all been concerned with the same kinds of themes. Moreover none of the
countries whose literature is studied in this book has a peculi-
arly unique national identity. All have similar socio-political
situations which were shaped by the collision of cultures during
colonisation, the quest for independence during the fifties and,
presently, ethnic conflict, tension between the urban and rural
sectors and, above all, underdevelopment.

This latter state of affairs has turned out to be not only the
source of a common theme for creative writers from many parts
of the continent but also, according to Clive Wake, a further in-
centive to them to function increasingly as judges and teachers
rather than simply as recorders or interpreters of their societies.
He suggests that

> independence has brought with it new problems with which
> the writer, the intellectual, the commentator must concern
> himself – the need to build nations that are 'one and
> indivisible' and to deal with the enormous social and
> economic problems associated with underdeveloped coun-
> tries. In nineteenth century Europe, when nationalism was
> to the foremost as it is in modern Africa, there were writers
> deeply committed to the idea that literature must contri-
> bute to the common good, but with this difference: Europe
> even then did not lack educated people to cope with its
> problems, so that the writer could be more of an observer
> than one personally implicated in public affairs. . . . Africa
> is desperately short of trained people and intellectuals, so
> that nearly everyone is engaged in public affairs, even
> though it may not always be in the glamorous ministerial
> roles. The modern African writer has, therefore, deeply
> impressed on him his duty to his country and the need to
> contribute to its growth by his writing.[6]

As will be seen in succeeding chapters, creative African

writers do indeed see themselves as writing seriously and not impartially about the nature and rules of their societies. One of their most pertinent observations is that, at the present time, politicians, the literati, bureaucrat-professionals and women are the major social actors. Of these, the politicians have by far been the dominant group in the post-colonial period. This is a tendency most of the writers deplore. They point out that the long-run effect of this dominance is alienation of the other actors from participation in the social system, resulting in a stagnation that virtually denies the ideology of the independence movements.

At present the literati do not play a leadership role since they are of the West in part, a fact which leads to loss of legitimacy among the general population. This is freely admitted by the creative writers. The literati are, however, together with the bureaucrat-professionals, perceived by the writers as the future socio-political leaders. Similarly the idea that African women never played significant roles in society in past eras is rejected in this literature. Women are seen as crucial actors in the modernising process, although their liberation from traditional roles often leads to alienation.

African creative writers see the tension between the rural and urban sectors, and the conflict between the communal and the individual ethic, as the dominant areas of strain for both the individual and the society as well. They suggest that while it is possible for the individual ethic to flourish in the urban sector, the communal ethic still dominates the rural sector. Yet in terms of social identity, aspects of both existences are desirable. The literature points out this paradox. It is recognised that until the tension is resolved, the political system which seeks to modernise society will in general fail. In this setting political parties and governments are 'seasonal' in nature in the sense that they do not provide linkages which join the two sectors of society together.

When the writers deal with independence, Pan-Africanism and the historical role of black peoples, they seek to define a cultural identity in the world. An important aspect of this attempt is the re-evaluation of the process of colonisation. This process, the literature points out, took place without the explicit co-operation of the indigenous people. It was executed by missionaries, traders and administrators, in that order of importance. Social change, too, during the colonial period was introduced by foreigners and perpetuated by the traditionally marginal groups and people. But in the future, social change will be effected by introducing a greater degree of participation in the socio-political system – particularly on the part of the rural sector – and by the establishment of the literati and the bureaucrat-professionals as the dominant social actors.

It should be stressed that the literature does not concern itself particularly with how these changes are going to be brought about, nor is it necessary that it does so in order to serve as a source of social and political theory. In their expression of preferences for certain outcomes over others, the writers are acting within their roles as recorders, interpreters and especially judges of the society of which they are a part. To the extent that they offer choices and criticisms of social phenomena, their ideas have a clear social and political relevance. All literature in the African context tends to function as a kind of social commentary. The artist creates art based on the ideas and problems which exist in his own particular society. This is one level on which the construction of social and political theory based on literature can be justified.

2 The Social and Political Nature of African Writing

There is another dimension to the whole question of the derivation of social theory from literature, and this pertains particularly to the work of African writers. It is the argument that in African societies art has traditionally been highly functional, and the contemporary African writer identifies with this tradition. Roy Sieber writes that

> Traditional African art for the most part was more closely integrated with the other aspects of life than those which might be purely aesthetic. Art for art's sake – as a governing aesthetic concept – seems not to have existed in Africa. Indeed the more closely an art form is related to a major non-aesthetic aspect of culture such as religion, the more distant it is from such separatist philosophical concepts.[1]

There is evidence that this attitude toward African art is not lost to the 'modern' artist. Austin J. Shelton points out that the Society of Nigerian Authors, in replying to Martin Tucker's 1962 argument that African novelists were over-communal and insufficiently individualistic in what they portrayed, were moving back to the traditional African perception of the artist and his role in society. In making such a response, he says,

> the Nigerian authors in effect reasserted a traditional attitude toward art as socially functional rather than aesthetically pleasing. One is thus justified in pursuing the study of modern literary works by Africans as expressions of attitudes and values related to tradition, contact and change.[2]

From this point of view the studying of literature in order to arrive at socio-political theory may be justified by the fact that

9

the 'modern' writers seek to continue a cultural attitude. They are socially committed and therefore write with this commitment in mind, because it has been the tradition of their culture to perceive the artist not as an individual but rather as a value creator and integrator. The African writer is, in Mugo Gathern's words, a 'child of two worlds'.[3] Though 'modern' in outlook, his perception of traditional African culture is positive and he is aware that he has to synthesise what was – and has been denied by the colonial situation – with what is now. In this process characters and situations, because they straddle two cultures, are used for snythesis. Thus Michael Dei-Anang, the leading Ghanaian poet, can write

> I love to dwell in the past
> Among the ruins of long ago
> Admiring and praising
> Correcting and building
> Among the ruins of long ago[4]

Clearly the writer views this as a positive function, not as a role which implies the irresolution of a person caught with each leg in a different civilisation.

In addition to synthesising two variant cultures – an integrative function that has traditionally been exercised by the artist in Africa – creative writers argue that they must also help the African view his past – and therefore his present and future as well – in perspective. It is a consensus among Africans that the colonial interlude constituted a denial of their past culture. Chinua Achebe, the Nigerian novelist, bluntly states:

> ... that African peoples did not hear of culture for the first time from Europeans; that their societies were not mindless but frequently had a philosophy of great depth and value and beauty, that they had poetry and above all, they had dignity. It is this dignity that many African peoples lost in the colonial period, and it is this that they must regain. ... The writer's duty is to help regain this by showing them in human terms what happened to them, what they lost.[5]

Furthermore, Achebe continues,

If I were God, I would regard as the very worst our acceptance – for whatever reason – of racial inferiority. It is too late in the day to get worked up about it or to blame others, much as they may deserve such blame and condemnation. What we need to do is to look back and try and find out where we went wrong, where the rain began to beat us. . . .

Here then is an adequate espouse – to help my society regain belief in itself and put away the complexes of the years of denigration and self-abasement. . . . The writer cannot expect to be excused from the task of re-education and regeneration that must be done. In fact he should march right in front. . . . I would be quite satisfied if my novels (especially the ones I set in the past) did no more than teach my readers that their past – with all its imperfections – was not one long night of savagery from which the first European acting on God's behalf, delivered them.[6]

Thus the beginning of the writers' erudition of what was and what is to be in terms of socio-political values must be rooted in the reconstruction of the past.

Owing to the peculiar nature of our situation, it would be futile to try and take off before we have prepared our foundations. We must first set the scene which is authentically African, then what follows will be meaningful and deep. This I think is what Aime Cesaire meant when he said that the shortcut to the future is via the past.[7]

This same kind of concern by the writer for teaching those who live in the present about their past and their possibilities in the future is stressed by Abioseh Nicol in the introductions to his two collections of stories, *The Truly Married Woman and Other Stories,* and *Two African Tales.*[8]

But the writer should not dwell only in the past. This is merely a transitional stage in which he must prepare the ground for the present and the future. It is only a stage for comprehension of the values with which he must judge and recommend the choices for the present and the future. For example; one of the writer's main functions in the past, according to Achebe, was to expose colonial injustices. But now a new situation has arisen.

Should we keep at the old theme of racial injustice (sore as it still is) when new injustices have sprouted around us? I think not. For just as it was appropriate in pre-independence days for Mabel Segun to write about the white man's 'bulldozers trampling on virgin ground in blatant violation,' even so it is urgent today for another Nigerian, John Ekwere, to add a 'Rejoinder'

> Now no more the palefaced strangers
> With unhallowed feet
> The heritage of our fathers profane
> Now no missioned benevolent despots
> Bull-doze on unwilling race;
> No more now the foreign hawks
> On alien chickens prey
> But we on us![9]

Some Western writers feel that the call for a reconstructing of the past and affirmation of the present with delineation of choices for the future has resulted in an alliance of the writer with the State, thereby impairing the ability of the writer to function independently in his criticism of the injustices perpetrated by the State. They question the entire nature and quality of this relationship and ask whether the socio-political involvement of the writer might impair his attempts to

> . . . probe into society, and try to capture its conflicts and tensions and in doing this with care and diligence to speak for the voiceless many.[10]

The majority of the African writers, however, seem to reject this view. They insist that the creative person in Africa has always functioned in a dual capacity as partly identified with and partly clearly separate from the sources of power and control within his society. Particularly now, when developments in the African political situation continue to point in an increasingly authoritarian direction, it is argued that the writer must go back to the tradition where

> the artist has always functioned in African society – as the record of mores and experience of his society *and* as the voice of vision in his own time.[11]

We have seen that African creative writers see their works as part of the task of creating viable societies from the cultural chaos of the colonial period. Thus they are involved in the re-creation of the identity of a society as they make choices and affirmations concerning what was and what should be. When we examine their works as a whole we can begin to find out something about the nature of their socio-political ideas. The remaining chapters of this book are devoted to that attempt.

Part Two: Group and Individual Identity in the African Context

3 The Literati[1]

Ulli Beier has written that

> It is one of the greatest ironies of history that the great quest
> for a new African identity comes from French West Africa
> and not from British West Africa. The French have de-
> stroyed far more African traditions than the British and have
> been far more successful in assimilating Africans to their
> European way of life. The British with their system of 'indi-
> rect rule' have left many traditional African institutions
> intact.[2]

But this is only part of the story. From another point of view the
phenomenon may not be as ironical as it seems. Perhaps
because of the French policy of assimilation, the literati of that
country's former holdings in Africa have been able to evolve a
clear identity in their dissent from these alien and omnipresent
philosophical and socio-political systems. The literati in the
former English colonies, on the other hand – precisely because
of the indirect and incomplete nature of the acculturation process they were subjected to – have suffered a continual crisis in
their quest for identity both during and after the colonial
period.

Two decades ago that quest was embodied in the all-
consuming task of achieving independence, and the literature
of the period argued that it was only through wresting the
instruments of government from the coloniser that the literati
could begin to have an identity rooted in the past.

> We have ruled ourselves before
> Though in a much more simple world
> And if your heart is sound and strong,
> You may triumph where we faltered
> And avoid the mocking pity

> Of the man who, in his heart
> Curses and despises you
> You deserve self-government now,
> But you must avoid its dangers
> If you want to make it work,
> Do not fall prey to daily
> Fear of death, and sudden death.
> Try amid the blood and passion,
> To discern a fitting answer
> To the cry:
> 'Self-governing what?
> Self-governing whom?'[3]

The idea that intellectuals had to participate in the struggle for independence and at the same time in the recreation of an indigenous culture in order to replace the culture of the West when it inevitably came to a violent end appears in other works in a more existential vein.

> What have we to offer, we
> Fruit of an unwise copulation between witches?
> The whole earth both its good and ill
> And all that's been usurped by magic fraud
> Leaving us with only our hate,
> The undying patience of the truly primitive
> The solid passion of the wholly vital
> And when your fine ingenuities
> Have toppled you back again to rubble
> We Calibans will inherit the earth.[4]

Yet even during the colonial period, and up to the present time, the literati have not been able to totally reject everything that was associated with the colonial system. Particularly striking is their susceptibility to many of the values implicit in the colonial way of thinking. There are Africans, for example, who refuse to admit that an African can be 'as good as' the white man. Consider this statement by Byeloh, an old-type government Minister, about the new and competent African civil servant:

But that John Hayford, now God why should I hate him so, when he's so useful to me? But I just can't help myself. He has all the wiles and brains of a white man. But his skin being black as mine, I'm damned if I'll admit he's superior to me. The white man taught me to honor the white man. I see no harm in that. It is not so hard to admit a white man is one's superior. When I go into a white man's presence, I not only feel inferior, I *know* it's proper for him to be superior to me. That's why as a Minister I refused to have a white man as my Permanent Secretary. I just couldn't have brought myself to feel I was *his* boss in *my* Ministry. And damn it all, it's be [sic] damn awkward to catch oneself answering one's own secretary as Sir. . . . But John Hayford now. He's no white man. Yet everyone admits he's cleverer than any white man in the service. Why should that be? After all he can't be better than a white man, cleverer – better? . . .[5]

No less troubling to many Africans is the question of the material comforts introduced by the Europeans and the extent to which those Africans who can afford to have the right to avail themselves of them. Some members of the literati, far from worrying about their identity or their role in society, have jumped into the world so to speak and acquired the trappings of wealth by any devious means open to them. The ambivalence and pangs of conscience that often accompany such a decision, however, are aptly expressed by Odili in Chinua Achebe's *A Man of the People*. After buying a car he states:

I could not help thinking also of the quick transformations that were such a feature of our country, and in particular of the changes of attitude in my own self. I had gone to the University with the clear intention of coming out again after three years as a full member of the privileged class whose symbol was the car. So much did I think of it in fact that, as early as my second year, I had gone and taken out a driver's license and even made a mental note of the make of car I would buy. . . . But in my final year I had passed through what I might call a period of intellectual crisis brought on partly by my radical Irish lecturer in history and partly by someone who five year earlier had been by all accounts a fire-eating president of our Students Union. He was now an ice-cream-eating Permanent Secretary in the Ministry of Labor and Production and had not only become one of the wealthiest and most corrupt landlords in Bori but was reported in the Press as saying that trade-union leaders should be put in detention. He had become for us a classic example of the corroding effect of privilege. . . . Many of us vowed then never to be corrupted by bourgeois privileges of which the car was the most visible symbol in our country. And now here I was in this marvellous little affair eating the hills like yams – as Edna would have said. I hoped I was safe; for a man who avoids danger for years and then gets killed in the end has wasted his case.[6]

Not only has Odili bought a car but the party of intellectuals, ironically called the Common Peoples Party, which Odili joined not because he had a social conscience but because the corrupt Minister Nanga had seduced his girl friend, accepts bribes from other political parties to refrain from fighting them. The leader of the 'intellectual' party ironically asks Odili: 'Now you tell me how you propose to fight such a dirty war without soiling your hands a little.'[7] Freddie, a character in Cyprian Ekwensi's *Jagua Nana*, who is virtuous in the sense that he transcends tribal and national differences to marry a girl from Sierra Leone, falls when he categorically states: 'I wan' money quick-quick; an' politics is de only hope.'[8]

African intellectuals are unsure whether to remain within an essentially European frame of reference or to create new and opposing systems perhaps patterned on elements of the traditional way of life. Yet even here there is uncertainty as to which elements of the traditional culture can be incorporated into a new structure and which, because of the colonial interlude, the intellectuals are now no longer willing to accept. The attitude of many of the literati toward manual labour is interesting in this context because it not only illustrates how far many of them have grown from the values of their ancestors but also how the new values they create can be of positive or negative influence in the society of which they are a part. William Conton writes

The Sagresa school had tried to teach us a trade, but so strongly did public opinion outside the school hold the view that even a starving professional [read literati] was nearer to the kingdom of heaven than the most successful artisan, that none of us took these attempts seriously.[9]

Although Conton goes on to point out that he lost this view abroad, there is no major African writer who has depicted an educated character indulging in manual labour of his own volition, or an educated person who does not aspire to a white-collar job. But by fostering a disdain for this kind of work, the literati may be creating an ideal that in the long run will be dysfunctional to the needs of a developing nation.

The African literati have guilt feelings stemming from the tribal values and precepts which they feel they must break in order to function as literati, but for which they are expected to pay in kind. This is the case with Obi Okonkwo, the hero of Chinua Achebe's *No Longer at Ease*. The Umofia Progressive Union feels that he is their *property* to be used as they see fit. The secretary to the said organisation,

> . . . Spoke of the great honour Obi had brought to the ancient town of Umuofia which could now join the comity of other towns in their march towards political irredentism, social equality and economic emancipation . . . The importance of having one of our sons in the vanguard of this march of progress is nothing short of axiomatic. Our people have a saying 'ours is ours, but mine is mine.' Every town and village struggles at this momentous epoch in our political evolution to possess that of which it can say: 'This is mine.' We are happy that today we have such an invaluable possession in the person of our illustrious son and guest of honour.[10]

The tragedy in terms of the identity and function of the society is that this is just one side of the coin. Obi who, we feel, should have known better, is forced to admit that

> . . . his people had a sizeable point. . . . They had taxed themselves mercilessly to raise eight hundred pounds to send him to England. Some of them earned no more than five pounds a month. He earned nearly fifty. They had wives and school-going children; he had none. After paying the twenty pounds he would have thirty left. And very soon he would have an increment which alone was as big as some peoples' salary. . . . What they did not know was that having laboured, in sweat and tears to enroll their kinsman among the

shining elite, they had to keep him up there. Having made him a member of an exclusive club whose members greet one another with 'How's the car behaving?', did they expect him to turn round and answer: 'I'm sorry, but my car is off the road. You see I couldn't pay my insurance premium?' That would be letting the side down in a way that was unthinkable.[11]

This is the dilemma of the pressure. The question is whether the literati allow themselves to become absorbed by the traditionalists by keeping the traditional obligations, or whether they wonder and muse and perhaps break away like Egbo in Soyinka's *The Interpreters*:

> Perfunctory doles towards the Union of Osa
> Descendants . . . messages between the old man
> and himself . . . all these hand built up ties
> surreptitiously . . . delegations too, to feel
> him out sent by Egbo Onosa as he knew quite
> well – identity, they said, you were destined . . .
> all these and much more . . . his own overwhelming
> need to retain that link with some out-of-the-rut
> existence . . . illicit pleasure at the thought that
> a kingdom awaited him whenever he wanted it . . .
> And he only plunged again into the ancient, psychic
> life of still sediments, muttering, how long will the
> jealous dead remain among us![12]

But of even greater significance to the literati's search for identity is the question of whether those who *do* see a significant role for traditional values in a new and non-European framework will be allowed to reclaim their roots in the past, since through their proximity to the coloniser and their knowledge of his ways the intellectuals have in large part become alienated from their own people. They are 'exiles', according to George Awoonor Williams, and therefore

> The return is tedious
> And the exiled souls gather on the beach
> Arguing and deciding their future
> Should they return home
> And face the fences the termites had eaten

And see the dunghill that has mounted on their
birth place?
But their journey homeward done on the seascapes
roar
Their final strokes will land them on the
forgotten shores
They committed the impiety of self deceit
Slashed, cut and wounded their souls
And left the mangled remainder in manacles
Before the sacred altar, alongside the
sacrificial cock
Whose crow woke the night sleepers at dawn

.   .   .   .

At the stars' entrance the night revellers gather
To sell their chatter and inhuman sweat to the
gateman
And shuffle their feet in agonies of birth
Lost souls, lost souls, lost souls that are still
at the gate.[13]

The intellectuals constitute, in fact, an entirely new social class
both in their occupations and in their way of thinking, and they
are unfamiliar with the style of life of the traditionalist people
who in the economies of the new Africa are equivalent to
Marx's and Toynbee's proletariat. The poet Nwanodi sums up
the point best. He writes:

We fell into the river
Splashing the water
On the river weeds,
We heard the rushing of water
Smelt the offshore farmtime ashes
and heard the offshore farmtime songs
We moved with the currents
Showing kola-free teeth. . . .

But we have poured more wine
than the gods can drink
more than the soil can drink
and have become outcasts
dispersing the fishes

for which the baskets are laid
and the fishermen did not like us

We turned and left the spot
but softly his voice rings
The waters are yours
and the water's yours
we are mere beings
beggars for your kindness
Oh! water god
give us, oh give us,
your products for our care
Soon the evening will come
and we'll go home with our baskets
Let not those who sit
by the fire feel cold

We looked at each other,
Packing our things hastily
Fearing more curses on our heads

Suddenly the drums beat
and the blowing of horns
called on all to the open ground
as the sun
Falling into the sea
threw glowing rays on all

Thus we stood shivering
From the violation of many
that judge and mock
our inviolate temper;

They spat on our terelyne
and called us outcasts
We held hearts with lips;
We have wished for many things,
Thought of many seasons
More than the gods can grant.[14]

Thus the literati, pressured by the Western tradition to play
a leadership role in modern society yet yearning for the security
of a traditional life that is no longer entirely open to them, find

solace sometimes in self-pity and negativism:

> I am not the hero
> of my own history
> I am the spectator
> of my own tragedy
> Disbelieving in everything
> > I believe in nothing
> > Including myself
> > Including yourself
> To stop doubting
> Is to stop thinking
> > The doubtful mind will
> Make a hiatus of reasons
> > Not from scepticism
> But from a divided will.[15]

Many of the literati develop a nihilist philosophy like those of Sagoe or Sekoni in Soyinka's *The Interpreters*.[16] At best, the post-colonial system in which they must function – and which questions their very achievement of an identity – often leads to a marked spirit of individualism in the literature they produce. Thus one writer can state

> I will lie here alone,
> Forgetting experiences past,
> alone
> to say 'am born alone,'
> lie and dream of dreams to come –
> the fantasy of youth
> nursed in rain and sun.
>
> Now am born alone
> joy of ills and fear of health
> in the welling of threatening dawn –
> new child of mature thoughts –
> alone
> to say 'am born alone'
> I will wait here alone,
> sit and sip from the broken mug
> and eat from mortars half burnt
> by harmattan blaze

Born at twenty six!
It's too early – and late
to forget the things I know well
remembering only myself
lost in search for something,
something that does not exist.
But am born now to say
'My heart's mine only'

I will walk here alone,
Seeing the scenes I see. . . .[17]

This theme of the loneliness of the literati is shown in one of the earliest novelettes. In *When Love Whispers*,[18] written in 1947, Cyprian Ekwensi narrates the loneliness of Ike, who wants to marry across tribal lines, and how the parents on both sides oppose the marriage. When Ike goes to England to study law, his girl-friend Ashoka is seduced by one of his colleagues, who refuses to marry her. Ashoka is ultimately married to the local chief, who has lusted after her all along. Thus Ike, in pursuing the study of law, is deprived of the tranquility he would have achieved had he chosen to marry, and marry within his own tribe.

Note that the values the literati stand for are often defeated in the literary works by traditional values. In the Ekwensi novel, for example, the local chief marries the girl even though she has a child born out of wedlock, whereas the man responsible refuses in the name of the uncivility of the idea. Even more striking in depicting the conflict between values is Soyinka's play *The Lion and the Jewel*.[19] Lakunle, a village teacher (representing the literati in the setting), seeks to marry Sidi, but his arrogance and bombast are no match for the cunning traditional chief Baroka. Sidi, the village beauty, gets carried away by the fame brought to her by being photographed for a magazine. Although Lakunle quotes to her almost all of the 'Shorter Companion Dictionary', she is not interested but falls prey to Baroka when she believes the rumour he has spread that he is impotent. She goes to taunt him, but he seduces her and thus she is bound to marry him.

Many of the literati, in an attempt to compensate for feelings of defeat, loneliness and uncertainty, become involved in work for the national government as a means of creating for themselves a collective self-identity. Yet even in joining the government, when they have the interests of the country at heart, they are dominated by the politicians in what they do. They become victims of the structure of their society, which places more value on politicians and politics than on the literati and intellectual leadership. This is essentially the case presented by Achebe in *A Man of the People*. There is a slump in coffee prices. Because the political party's electorate is composed mainly of coffee farmers, this presents a crisis.

> The Minister of Finance at the time was a first rate economist with a Ph.D. in public finance. He presented to the Cabinet a complete plan for dealing with the situation. The Prime Minister said 'no' to the plan. He was not going to risk losing the election by cutting down the price paid to coffee planters at the critical moment. The National Bank should be instructed to print fifteen million pounds. Two-thirds of the Cabinet supported the Minister. The next morning the Prime Minister sacked them and in the evening he broadcast to the nation. He said the dismissed Ministers were conspirators and traitors who had teamed up with foreign saboteurs to destroy the new nation. . . . The *Daily Chronicle*, an official organ of the P.O.P., had pointed out in an editorial that the Miscreant Gang, as the dismissed ministers were now called, were all university people and highly educated professional men.
>
> Let us now and for all extract from our body-politic as a dentist extracts a stinking tooth all those decadent stooges versed in textbook economics and aping the white man's mannerisms and way of speaking. We are proud to be Africans. Our true leaders are not those intoxicated with their Oxford, Cambridge or Harvard degrees but those who speak the language of the people. Away with the damnable and expensive university education which only alienates the African from his rich and ancient culture and puts him above his people.[20]

Thus, inbuilt in the systems being evolved in many African countries is a strong bias against the literati. Perhaps to some extent the writers themselves are to blame for not having worked hard enough to propagate the ideas and roles of the literati in society. Consider the fact that of all the books and plays written since 1945 only one deals with university life *per se*. This is *Toads for Supper*, by U. Chikwuemeka Ike.[21] This novel details the life of an undergraduate, but it is noticeably lacking in concern for social problems and in elucidating the role of the university in shaping ideas with which to develop society. The only matters of concern to the undergraduates are their next meal and – of all things – whether or not they can foxtrot! Wole Soyinka also satirises the professors in African universities. Their only concerns are whether guests at their parties follow the Victorian custom of the compulsory retirement of the women upstairs; the gossip on how many pregnancies the college obstetrician has dug up; and another professor's[22] declaration that he never takes prostitutes home – only to his garage! In African literary works the conclusion seems to be that African universities fail to function as agents of change.

The only novel which specifically seeks to deal with the hardships and dangers of intellectual leadership is *The Voice* by Gabriel Okara.[23] Okolo, the hero – the names means voice – searches after 'it' but 'the elders, not wanting the people to hear',[24] stop him. He is banished by Chief Izongo who is advised to do so by a B.A., M.A., Ph.D., that is to say, a corrupt member of the literati. The writer makes it clear however that the elders and the chief, by acting in a corrupt way, are really going against tradition. 'Our fathers' insides always contained things straight. They did straight things. Our insides were also clean and we did the straight thing until the new time came. We can still sweep the dirt out of our house every morning.'[25] Having gone through all the tribulations and arguments for the primacy of state authority in an underdeveloped situation, and with the knowledge that had he kept quiet he would have acquired cars, women and liquor, Okolo (and perhaps the literati in general) is shown to have a dim prospect for the future when the author says of him 'If the masses haven't got *it* he will create *it* in their insides. He will plant *it*, make *it* grow in spite of Izongo's destroying words. He will uproot the fear in their insides and plant *it*. He will all these do if only . . . if only what?'[26]

There the question hangs. Perhaps it is the only realistic summary of the role of the African literati other than the statement by T. C. Nwosu's 'B. B.', who complains,

> Twenty pounds for a modest flat
> That breeds relations like a rat.
> Fifteen pounds for the loan of a car.
> That signals poverty weeping from afar.
> Ten pounds to the H.P. agent
> For the telly won on monthly rent.
> Six pounds to the overbearing creditor
> Who indulges such a chronic debtor.
> Five pounds for the weekend booze
> And the girls for the usual cruise.
> Two pounds ten for the ticking parasites
> That visit more often than bed bug bites
> One pound ten on football pools
> Won more often by the best fools.
> Pause and think on this subject
> Of monthly income and monthly budget.
> You only need to take a quick glance
> To see both will never balance.[27]

Perhaps it is no wonder that the literati are corrupted by money, which in a way provides one solution to their identity problem, although not as most of the writers would like. For, by allying themselves with the politicians, the literati do acquire some of the status roles and positions of influence not open to them as literati *qua* literati. But there is an equally strong current of opinion which holds that as intellectual leaders of their emergent societies the literati must pay by individual suffering, since

> What you suffer in your day
> Is the price you have to pay
> As you try to come to rest
> From the swaying free of change.[28]

That is to say, the intellectual leadership of the emergent societies depends, in the last analysis, on the integrity of the literati and on their not being swallowed up in the petty, mundane world of politics, money and loose women. Of course in the real world, the intellectuals are just as confused as the other categories since their societies are structured in such a way that all social categories are at the mercy of the economic and political forces eminating from outside the continent. Identity can only be forged if there is systematic ideology which denies the penetrative power of the international system. In the mid-1970s there are elements of thought which point toward the creation of such ideological orientation, but they are too scattered for us to analyse here.

4 The Bureaucrats and Professionals

The central fact in the depiction of professionals or bureaucrats in African literature is that they are mistrusted and out-manoeuvered by the politicians. Chief Nanga – Achebe's man of the people – bluntly tells his colleague in corruption, the Hon. T. C. Kobino: 'You know very well T. C. that you cannot trust these boys. That is why I always say that I prefer to deal with Europeans.'[1] In *One Man, One Matchet*, a novel by T. M. Aluko, Udo Akpan, a District Officer in a colonial setting, is frustrated in his administrative duties – the eradication of cocoa disease by cutting the trees, – by Benja-Benja, a semi-literate politician who agitates: 'What we in Ipaja want the government to do for us is not to cut down our cocoa trees. Government need not do this to demonstrate to us the power of the white man. We already know that.'[2] In another novel one of the characters, Lombe, is frozen in his job because the Ministry will never let him rise higher, since they have to maintain 'efficiency and integrity'[3] provided of course by foreigners! In Wole Soyinka's *The Interpreters*, Sekoni, an engineer assigned to the Ministry of Public Works, stammers that he is tired of

'. . . ssigning vouchers and llletters and b-b-bicycle allow-ances!'

Pandemonium, except for the practical chairman, calm and full of instant calculation. 'Just wait outside a moment, please, Mr Sekoni!

'Is he mad?'

'O mo tani?'

'Why do we employ these too-knows?'

'No, no, no', and the Chairman soothed them.

31

'He obviously needs a transfer. He is one of the keen ones.'

And to Ijioha Sekoni went, 'where you may work with your hands until your back blisters' and Sekoni built a small experimental power station. And the Chairman chuckled and said, 'I knew he was our man. Get me the expert.' Hot from his last lucrative 'evaluation' came the expatriate expert. Expatriate, therefore impartial.

'Constitute yourself into a one-man commission of enquiry and probe the construction of our power station at Ijioha which was built without estimates of approved expenditure.'

'Is it unsafe for operation', and he winked, a truly expert wink.

'That's the safest idea. You put it in technical language.'

And the expatriate expert came to Ijioha, saw and condemned.

And the Chairman read the report and said, 'That expert never fails me', salivating on the epithets, a wasteful expenditure, highly dangerous conditions, unsuitable materials, unsafe for operation.

'Bring me the write-off file', chortled the Chairman.

And the project was written off while parliament at question time resounded to 'the escapade of the made engineer'.

'Interdict him, shall we? Bring me form S/7 Interdiction of Senior Civil Servants and Confidential File Sekoni Chief Engineer-in-charge Ijioha.'

And the Chairman – for his subsidiary company registered in the name of his two-month-old niece had been sole contractor for Project Ijioha – cleaned out a few thousand in immediate compensation and filed claims for a few thousand more. 'I always say it, the write-offs pay better than fulfilled contracts.' And to Sekoni, 'the expert says that was junk, Engineer, junk'. And Sekoni, bewildered, repeating, 'J-j-j-junk? J-j-j-junk?'[4]

Unfortunately Sekoni had not been aware that he was being manipulated by the politician. Even worse, the villagers had been led to believe that 'electricity was a government thing' and 'when it got ready it would provide for them'. Thus Sekoni had been used by the politician for the latter's ends, which included manipulating the illiterate rural masses against the professional and well-meaning engineer.[5]

Even though the writers basically admire and praise the bureaucrats and professionals they depict them as having a major problem of identity and function which makes them susceptible to manipulation by the politicians. This is the failure of the bureaucrats and professionals to understand the 'ways of the ancestors' and to know when and how to introduce Western ideas into settings where they are not readily acceptable. Consider the teacher in Aluko's *One Man, One Wife*. He tries to dispute the existence of ghosts and the inherent superiority of the white man by stating: 'What the white man can do, we too can do. But we must first go to school.'[6] To which Joshua, a Christian church elder, dissents, by saying: 'Teacher you are black, I am black. Don't let us lie to each other. Even Christianity cannot explain certain mysterious things in this country. Even the white man's magic cannot explain these things. Teacher there are ghosts.'[7]

In this exchange the professional, playing the role of innovator, purveyor of new values, is willing to question even the fundamental identity of ghosts and thereby risk losing his identification with the people and his ability to initiate change. This failure is also expressed by Grandma Gbemi, a character in the same novel, when she utters the following incantation against lawyers and doctors:

'Lawyer! Lawyer!' Grandma Gbemi cried in distress. 'Shonponna m'Lord forbid that I should ever have anything to do with lawyers. They turn innocent people's cases round and send them to gaol. They are as bad as the doctors who cut open people's stomachs.'[8]

Udo Akpan and his friends, the doctors and lawyers, are similarly rejected in *One Man, One Matchet*.[9]

African people mistrust professionals partly because of the nature of their work. A doctor does not, of course, just cut up people for the fun of it, but does so in pursuit of what professional ethics demand. This is not to argue, however, that some professionals are not mistrusted and rejected by the people because they 'mis-practise' their professions. One lawyer, Chris, is rejected because he is a shyster in T. M. Aluko's *Kinsman and Foreman*.[10] Benjamin-Benjamin (Benja-Benja), an 'educated' shyster in T. M. Aluko's *One Man, One*

Matchet, is not only rejected but is also shot because he 'mis-practises' his profession. Udo Akpan, the District Officer explains to Stanfield, the English Officer he is replacing,

> Before you British came to this country with Pax Britannica, a citizen of proved anti-community activities like Benjamin-Benjamin was easily disposed of. He just vanished. . . . After we in the Administration had failed to rid ourselves of the curse that was Benjamin-Benjamin, an Ipaja man who had not heard of the British sense of fair play and justice, and in any case had no use for it, got rid of the common enemy. He did it in a moment. We had failed to do it in two years. . . . After Olowo had shot his enemy he did not want to live. He turned his own gun on himself. But we did not allow him to die . . . we concentrated on him the best medical attention in the country. And after this care and attention – we are going to hang him by the neck till he be dead![11]

Udo Akpan thus points out the two crucial problems of the bureaucrat-professional. On the one hand he feels he has to prove to the white man that he is worthy of his position, and on the other, he must operate under two conflicting codes in a social setting where he is rejected both by the coloniser and by his own people. Moreover he must challenge both systems. Thus Udo Akpan is sympathetic to the elimination of Benja-Benja and is willing to restructure the role of the bureaucrat in society in a way quite different from the traditional British con-ceptualisation. He categorically states:

> The British Civil Servant does not have to engage in politics because there are literally hundreds of thousands of fellow Britons who are outside the Civil Service and who are avail-able to engage in politics both at the national and the local government levels. The Civil Servant can therefore sit at his desk to carry out his own assignment, that of implementing policy decisions. . . . But here in this country the situation is sadly different. The best brains of this country are with a few exceptions all in the Civil Service. Can this country with its limited resources in educated man-power afford to have their mouths padlocked in the Civil Service while second-rate and sometimes semi-literate men are saddled with the very

important duty of legislating and taking executive decisions for the state? Can we not have a state of affairs where the civil servant can make his views known publicly on matters on which he is by qualification and experience competent to express his views?[12]

We have already pointed out that the politician, who is usually less qualified than the bureaucrat-professional, dominates the post-independence political and social situation, while the bureaucrat-professional is co-opted as an ally by the politician for economic and prestige purposes. A preference for social and political leadership by the intellectual-bureaucrat-professional is clearly articulated by the African writers but they point out that this is not yet the case. There are many reasons for this situation. Two have been touched upon already, namely, the failure of the professionals to adapt their innovations to the traditional setting, and also the fact that they are often, whether rightly or wrongly, mistrusted by the people. Part of the explanation for this mistrust is the non-discriminating attitude of the population in regarding 'being educated' as equivalent to 'rejecting the ways of the ancestors', and also in equating all educated persons with the few corrupt educated. Thus those who are educated are rejected because the Benja-Benja's are rejected.[13]

Another major reason for the inferior position of the bureaucrat-professional is the bias in African societies in favour of the politician. The politician 'brought' independence and thereby gained access to roles of power and status. The professional often stayed out of the nationalist movement because the colonial system would have victimised him.[14] He never acquired from the public, as the politician did, credit for having rid them of the white man. Today the politician, by controlling power and status positions, can manipulate the system to the extent that in purely economic terms he can 'buy' the bureaucrat-professional for his camp, or at least the bureaucrat-professional has to pay the politician homage if the former wants economic security in his career. In the novel *No Bride Price*, by David Rubadiri, Lombe never rises to the top of the civil service because foreigners are preferred by the insecure politicians at the top.[15] The Minister finally destroys Lombe because the latter refuses to yield a girl friend.[16]

Dan Kaybi, one of the characters in Cyprian Ekwensi's *Iska*, is a bureaucrat whose lack of identity generates problems of another sort. He is a young civil servant, who wants to marry across tribal lines. The parents on both sides disapprove. However, his Permanent Secretary approves – he regards this relic of tradition as just as irrelevant as Kaybi does. However, as Kaybi celebrates the authorisation by the Permanent Secretary, which insures his professional progress at least, he is knifed while trying to stop a fight between the youths of his tribe and those of his wife's tribe.[17] John Hayford, in Easmon's *The New Patriots*, is paid the 'highest' compliment by his incompetent Minister who tells him that 'He has all the wiles and brains of a white man.'[18] Yet we know that as a brilliant professional he cannot be comfortable working with an incompetent Minister who becomes a shaking mass of jelly in the presence of any white person. Obi Okonkwo, in Achebe's work *No Longer at Ease*, succumbs to economic pressures and accepts a bribe. Although he falls, what one should recognise is the pressure put on him by the civil service system to maintain the standards of the colonial bureaucrat in terms of cars, dress and ritual, and also the pressure from his own people on one who had a white man's job. All this, together with the personal loss of his mother and girl-friend, made him a supreme cynic.[19]

The army can be included in the bureaucrat-professional class, but unfortunately few writers have concerned themselves with the army. As a matter of fact no novel or play has been written with the army or the police playing a central role. This, one predicts, will not be the case in the future since there have in the recent past been 'enough' *coups d'état* to require analysis by the writers. It may be noted that Chinua Achebe in *A Man of the People* does mention the army but not as playing a significant role in the political process. His character states that it 'obliged us by staging a coup at that point and locking up every member of Government. The rampaging bands of election thugs had caused so much unrest that our young army officers seized the opportunity to take over.[20] It should be noted that Achebe stresses only the benevolent nature of the *coup d'état* and further that it is carried out by the young officers. He is suggesting perhaps that the old political order was supported by the older members of the army, that is by those who had moved from the colonial set-up into political, civil service or military careers, as contrasted with the newer, younger army men who seek to reshape the post-independence period.

Another treatment of the army is found in David Rubadiri's *No Bride Price*, which contains several key ideas. First there is a civilian organisation that works to bring the government to power. This organisation embraces the alienated educated who are debarred from work and who live the bar–cocktail–party route along with the seamier side of the top echelon of business and diplomacy.[21] The implication here is that the educated who cannot get into the system will ally with the army to throw out uneducated bureaucrats and politicians from public life. More interesting is the idea Rubadiri puts forward when he argues that Gombe, the 'father of independence' in this particular country and the one who had played the dominant political role in the ending of the colonial situation, is the head of the underground organisation which allies itself with the army to bring about the *coup*. Rubadiri argues that the 'father of the nation' had quit the government because it had become corrupt and his interest in the new order is to achieve good government.[22] This suggests that the only way to get 'good', that is to say non-corrupt, government is to use the young educated and the military. The military leader puts his case for the *coup* in the following way:

> This is General Masauko of the National Army. I have today removed the power from the government. This was made necessary for the good of the nation. Over the past three years much harm has been caused by the people you elected to rule you. Not only has there been corruption, murder and injustice but their policies and love of power had forced them to use all means to destroy the people. A whole generation of young people has been turned into monsters, trained to be destroyers of lives and destroyers of our formerly simple and great people. Foreign killers from abroad for reasons of their own took on the responsibility of performing those tasks and the nation now will have to live through a generation of citizens whose values no longer exist but simply function blindly for the ambitions of a handful of people to whom the only

achievement was power and the retention of power.[23]

The ideas expressed here are important because they point to the army as the saviour of the nation from corruption and to the rejection of the domination of the politicians. It should be noted that Lombe, the civil servant, is rehabilitated into the new order. Perhaps the future may see more and more of this kind of alliance between the political bureaucracy, the intellectuals looking to the African past for the major values of society, and the military who by their very definition are professionals. This seems to be confirmed by the spate of *coups* and attempted *coups* since 1960 throughout the African continent.

5 The Politicians and the Political Process

> Ism to ism for ism is ism
> Of ism and isms on absolute-ism
> To demonstrate the tree of life
> Is sprung from broken peat
> And we the rotted bark, spurned
> When the tree swells its pot
> The mucus that is snorted out
> When Kongi's new race blows
> And more. . . .[1]

The 'politician' is relatively new in African culture. He is older than the intellectual but younger than the bureaucrat because the British, with their emphasis on the civil service, stressed administration at the expense of both politics and creative thought. The colonial politicians came to flower during the fifties as agitators for independence, often by giving rein within themselves,

. . . to precisely those urges and inclinations which people of good breeding the world over try to keep in check – the inclination to draw the derision and scorn of others upon ones rulers for example; and the urge to acquire as much personal power and wealth as possible. . . . Unfortunately as the colonies advance[d] toward self-government, the African politicians with whom the British officials came into contact, and are inevitably compared, have usually been much less well prepared for their careers. Politics is unfortunately still widely regarded as a profession something less than honorable in Africa. . . .[2]

The colonial politician was primarily an agitator, and to the extent that there was scarcely a dearth of issues to agitate over, he never really learned how to develop a programme, articulate it and become accountable to the people. In fact, he never worried, like the English theoretician Burke, about whether he was to be instructed by the people and act as their agent or simply do as he pleased. The issue of accountability never arose because the very nature of the system was such that the rewards for agitation were high, and there was no room for questions of responsibility either on the part of the politician or on the part of the people. This is why the traditionalist Chief Ozuomba, in Egbuna's *Wind Versus Polygamy*, can state: 'Can't you see that these mushrooming politicians, who are nothing but a bunch of Europeans in black skins, are determined to prostitute our culture, our pride, our dignity.'[3] He is speaking of the fact that the politician is often a virtual outsider to the traditional culture, and his values are animated mostly by hopes of self-aggrandisement, not by considerations of how he fits into the society.

In African literary works the politician is generally depicted as the one person above all who, during the independence period, exploits the people. In the crucial struggle towards cultural identity and national unification, therefore, his outstanding defect is his failure to strive for cultural values that are higher than money and materialism. The politician impedes rational decision-making in the whole of society and thus retards development. In the novel *Jagua Nana* we find the following statements by Jagua, the prostitute:

> No Freddie. I no wan' you to win. . . . Politics not for you, Freddie. You got education. You got culture. You're a gentleman an' proud. Politics be game for dog. And in dis Lagos, is a rough game. De roughest game in de whole worl'. Is smelly an' dirty an' you too clean an' sweet.[4]

In the play *The New Patriots*, a Chief Justice gives the following estimate of what politicians are: '. . . The politicians themselves need no training or apprenticeship in their craft; *they* gravitate into politics like rats into a sewer and swim around quite naturally in the filth.'[5]

In the novel *A Man of the People* we are informed that those in power

> . . . a handful of us – the smart and the lucky and hardly ever the best – had scrambled for the one shelter our former rulers left and had taken it over and barricaded themselves in. And from within they sought to persuade the rest through numerous loudspeakers that the first phase of the struggle had been won and that the next phase – the extension of our house – was even more important and called for new and original tactics; it required that all arguments should cease and the whole people speak with one voice and that any more dissent and argument outside the door of the shelter would subvert and bring down the whole house.[6]

In the quest of 'building the one house' the politician accepts only himself as master designer and builder with the help of money. Jagua asks Uncle Taiwo where the money he spends comes from. Uncle Taiwo, the suave politician with a Pontiac, answers:'Is party money. I give dem de money like dat, so them kin taste what we goin to do for them, if they vote us into power.'[7] Uncle Taiwo, for all his kindness, is coarse, believing only in the power of money.[8]

In the play *The New Patriots*, Momoh Seisay, a member of the government, enlightens us further as to the values to which the politician aspires. He states:

> . . . Oh, Lord, what a beautiful and simple system of government a dictatorship is. That's what we need in this country. Leader of opposition – lock him up. Gag your trade union leaders with gold or fear. As for the press which thinks abuse of Government is the only freedom of speech, either control it absolutely or hold the bribe of a Government job like a carrot in front of those donkeys who call themselves newspaper editors.[9]

Such tactics are applied by the politicians against the intellectuals with a finesse that would astound a Machiavelli. Consider the case of Sagoe, a journalist returned from the States, in Soyinka's *The Interpreters*. He goes for an interview for a newspaper job. (The interviewing board, like all other boards in the country we are told, is the enclave of the politicians on a downward skid. Their compatriots cushion their fall by appointing them to a government board.) When Sagoe walks into the room the only question asked is

> 'Why do you want this job?'
>
> 'I don't know', Sagoe said.
>
> The carcass of the Managing Director swelled, spurted greasy globules of the skin in extreme stages of putrefication [sic] and burst out in an unintelligible stream through the ruptured throat, 'Do you think we have come here to tolerate your cocky impudence! You small boy, you come here begging for a job. . . .'
>
> 'I have not come to beg.'
>
> 'Don't talk when I am talking otherwise just get out. We want the kind of person who is going to respect his superior, not conceited boys of your type. Suppose you are not begging, who is interested in that? Your betters are begging my friend, go sit down. . . . Please go from my sight. . . . These small fries, they all think they are popularly in demand, just because they have a degree.'[10]

No interpretation of the thinking of this person and his values is necessary.

African writers are clear in their assessment of the role and values of the politician in post-independence Africa. But what of political parties, the electoral process and electoral techniques in general? What do the writers say about these phenomena and about how they are viewed by the various groups in African society, including the politicians themselves?

Since the politicians perceive their public duty as basically that of acquiring and perpetuating power, it logically follows that they cultivate only 'primitive loyalty',[11] that is, loyalty to the clan and the tribe which make up their constituency and not to a party or to overriding political or social programmes. Thus our man of the people, Nanga, seeks to recruit Odili into his entourage:

> By the way, Odili, I think you are wasting your talent here [teaching in a village]. I want you to come to the capital and take up a strategic post in the civil service. We shouldn't leave everything to the highland tribes. My secretary is from there,

our people must press for their fair share of the national cake![12]

There is the further suggestion that this is the view not only of the politicians but rather of the majority of the people as well. Odili, a member of the literati in *A Man of the People*, states

> My father's attitude to my political activity intrigued me a lot. . . . He took the view (without expressing it in so many words) that the mainspring of political action was personal gain, a view which, I might say, was much more in line with the general feeling in the country than the high-minded thinking of fellows like Max and I.[13]

As is pointed out in James Ngugi's *A Grain of Wheat*,

> Parties *per se* mean nothing. Nearly everybody was a member of the Party, but nearly nobody could say with accuracy when the Party was born. To most people, especially the younger generation, the Party had always been there, a rallying centre of action. It changed names, leaders came and went, but the Party remained.[14]

It is in other words an amorphous thing which takes different shapes at different times for different reasons. In the winning of elections it is not the party that is of primary importance but the money to be gained. The technique requires also the convincing of 'a large clan [who] make up nearly half of the electorate'.[15] Above all it is necessary for the politician to know how to delude the public. For example when people demand the paving of a road, Ekunyah, the perfect politician in James Henshaw's *Medicine for Love*, explains his procedure for duping his constituents on this and other issues:

> The road will cost several thousand pounds. But wait . . . tell them I shall build the road . . . hire about a hundred drums of tar. Line them along the road. . . . Then hire several loads of sand and heap the sand at suitable intervals along the road. An impression must be given that the road work is starting any moment now. Most important of all, bring this road development scheme to the notice of the newspapers. Don't forget to report in the newspapers the contribution I have made to the church organ fund . . . think what it will mean

when all the women in the church whisper it around that
Ewia Ekunyah has paid a hundred and twenty pounds
towards the church's new organ fund. . . . How many beggars have we in this constituency? . . . What percentage of
the total electorate? . . . If all the beggars were to vote against
me in a block, would it make a difference to the results?[16]

Since the answer is no, the beggar is sent away without any
dole!

Another important aspect of political parties as pictured in
African literary works is that not only do their activities exacer-
bate tribal animosities but also their very existence disrupts the
family and the tribe. This is the lament of Ocol's wife, Lawino,
in p'Bitek's *Song of Lawino*:

> I do not understand
> The new political parties.
> They dress differently,
> They dress in robes
> Like the Christian diviner-priests
> But Ocol treat his brother
> As if they are not relatives.[17]

Lawino's husband and brother-in-law fight each other from
two different political party bases. The alleged ability of the
parties to bring unity, development, and the new culture to the
people is therefore questioned by the traditionalist Lawino. She
wonders:

> The new parties have split the homestead
> As the battle axe splits the skull!
>
> .   .   .   .
>
> Is this the unity of uhuru
> Is this the Peace
> That Independence brings?[18]

Then, concerning the motivation for joining the parties, she
says:

> The stomach seems to be
> A powerful force
> For joining the political parties,
> Especially when the purse

In the trouser pocket
Carries only the coins
With holes in the middle
And no purple notes
Have ever been folded in it
And especially for those who
Have never tasted honey from childhood,
And those who grew up
Fatherless or motherless
And those with no sure jobs.[19]

Thus we are told in a modern praise song[20] that the motivation for joining the various parties is what one can get for his stomach, and that basically it is only outcasts and other riff-raff who take to the parties seriously.

This riff-raff or fringe element of the parties includes a very interesting group of people generally referred to as 'the wild ones'. The wild ones are the thugs or Youth Wingers who attach themselves to every politician. They are under his pay to sing his praise,[21] act as errand boys in tasks like running to buy sweets and soda for the 'humble citizens',[22] and above all fight, maim, and even kill the members of the opposition. The thug element in the parties is so strong that they can actually hold the parties hostage, and in several countries they have facilitated the take-over of governments. Achebe, in *A Man of the People*, describes how the fighting between rival gangs ultimately leads to the overthrow of the government:

> The people had nothing to do with the fall of our Government. What happened was simply that unruly mobs and private armies having tasted blood and power during the election had got out of hand and ruined their masters and employers. And they had no public reason whatever for doing it.[23]

What of the fabled people as actors in the political process? They are pictured in the literature as being simply apathetic and cynical, believing that they have to take whatever falls to them. To wit, 'Honourable Chief Nanga is my brother and he is what white man call V.I.P. . . . me na P.I.V. – Poor Innocent Victim. . . . Yes me na P.I.V. . . . . A bottle of beer cost only five shillings. Chief Honourable Nanga has the money – as of today.'[24] Social concern over problems such as corruption and the rampages of wild ones means nothing to this fellow who is thirsting only after a beer. Thus when

> . . . political commentators [say] that it was the supreme cynicism [of the politicians] that inflamed the people and brought down the Government . . ., that is sheer poppycock. The people themselves, as we have seen, had become even more cynical than their leaders and were apathetic in the bargain. 'Let them eat,' was the people's opinion, 'after all when the white men used to do all the eating did we commit suicide? Of course not.
>
> And where is the all powerful white man today?
> He came, he ate and he went.
>
> But we are still around. The important thing then is to stay alive; if you do, you will outlive our present annoyance. The great thing as the old people have told us is reminiscence; and only those who survive can have it. Besides if you survive, who knows it may be your turn to eat tomorrow. Your son may bring home your share. . . .[25]

Achebe is suggesting here that the populace does not *really* understand the stakes involved in pitting their kind of orientation against public wealth. Perhaps our traditionalist woman Lawino is right when she points out that women do not yodel and ululate in political rallies because they like or understand what is said but rather

> They shout and make ululations
> Because they are tired
> Tired of the useless talk
> Tired of the insults
> And the lies of
> The speakers.
> They shout and raise their hands
> Not because they understand,
> But because they do not understand
> The many foreign words.[26]

Although the politician is almost universally damned by the various groups in African societies, it is from the intellectuals and from African writers in particular that their strongest criticism comes. This condemnation dates from the early fifties when Dr R. E. G. Armattoe broke with Kwame Nkrumah over the way in which Ghana should be run when the latter became Prime Minister. Armattoe wrote in the poem 'Servant-Kings':

> Leave them alone,
> Leave them to be
> Men lost to shame
> To honour lost!
> Servant kinglets,
> Riding to war
> Against their own
> Watched by their foes
> Who urge them on,
> And laugh at them! . . .[27]

In the poem *They Said* he pinpoints the criticism of a fellow intellectual-turned-politician and therefore become corrupt in the following words,

> They said
> You may take donkeys to water
> But you can't make them drink;
> You may teach monkeys to chatter
> But you can't make them sing;
> You may soak a cork in water
> But you can't make it sink;
> You call him the Prime Minister
> And would that make him think?
> They asked.[28]

This criticism of all politicians has continued in African literature. In the play *Kongi's Harvest* the criticism is depicted by the exchange between the Organising Secretary of Kongi's Party and the Third and Fourth Aweri's – Kongi's official 'Disputants' (a simpler word is stooges).

Organizing Secretary. All we want is some way of persuading King Danlola to bring the New Yam to Kongi with his own hands. . . . Kongi desires that the King perform all his customary spiritual functions, only this time that he perform them to him, our Leader. Kongi must preside as the Spirit of Harvest, in pursuance of the Five Year Development Plan.

Fourth. An inevitable stage in the process of power reversionism. . . .

Organizing Secretary. And the key word, Kongi insist, must be – Harmony. We need that to counter the effect of the bomb-throwing. Which is one of the reasons why the culprits of that outrage will be hanged tomorrow.

Fourth. An exercise in scientific exorcism – I approve. . . .

Organizing Secretary. Every Ismite must do his Mite.
. . . Ismite-is-Might. . . .

Fourth. It needs a live person to make even a symbolic act of capitulation.

Third. Especially when harmony is the ultimate goal. The ultimate goal.

Fourth. I think I see something of the Leader's vision of this harmony. To replace the old superstitious festival by a state ceremony governed by the principle of Enlightened Ritualism. It is therefore essential that the Oba Danlola, his highest opponent, appear in full antiquated splendor surrounded by his Aweri Conclave of Elders who, beyond the outward trappings of pomp and ceremony and a regular supply of snuff, have no other interest in the running of the state. . . . The period of isolated saws and wisdom is over, superseded by a more systematic formulation of comprehensive philosophies – *our* function, for the benefit of those who still do not know it. . . . And Danlola, the retrogressive autocrat, will with his own hands present the Leader with the New Yam, thereby acknowledging the supremacy of the State over his former areas of authority, spiritual and secular. From then on, the State will adopt towards him and to all similar institutions the policy of glamourized fossilism.[29]

Thus through satire the writer points out the incongruity between the new political leaders who are seen as inhuman, totalitarian and essentially egomaniacs, as opposed to the figure of the traditional leader Oba Danlola who is portrayed sympathetically as a humane person in the play.

Other characterisations of Ministers are just as biting. Consider the Minister of Consolation in Cyprian Ekwensi's *Beautiful Feathers*! He heads a ministry which 'was founded as a *sympathetic* gesture, a kind of *Universal* Aunt.'[30] As the Perennial Secretary, who is white and remains in his position only as a personal stooge, tells us; '*Our True Speaker*, Mr Malu, is another politician.' Wilson Mativo writes of how the politician swoops down into the rural areas, finds a meeting by his rival in progress, gets his 'wild ones' to break the rival's car, buys sweets and soda for the people, and drives away at once with a convoy of body-guards to live in the city until the next election.[31] It is not only that the writers depict their own hatred of the politician. They also put such opinions in the mouths of numbers of other professional groups. Kachigwe in *No Easy Task* has one of the characters say this about the politician Dube: ' "Do you admire his brains?" "Me," he said it as if I had asked him to love a snake. "He is a politician, and politicians are a tribe of their own. I am a journalist, not a politician." '[32]

To argue that politicians are a tribe of their own is in the African context to define them as outside society – pariah to all others in their values and their interests. Thus when Gikonyo, in Ngugi's novel *A Grain of Wheat*, wants to buy land from a departing European, but is refused a loan by a Member of Parliament who then goes on to buy the same farm himself, we know that the Member of Parliament is looking after the interests of his own tribe – the politician tribe.[33] We can therefore understand the feeling of alienation by other non-political tribes when George Awoonor-Williams writes,

> And our songs are dying on our lips.
> Standing at hell-gate you watch those who seek admission
> Still the familiar faces that watched and gave you up
> As the one who had let the side down.
> 'Come on, old boy, you cannot dress like that'
> And tears well in my eyes for them
> Those who want to be seen in the best company
> Have abjured the magic of being themselves
> And in the new land we have found
> The water is drying from the towel.
> Our songs are dead and we sell them dead to the other side

Reaching for the stars we stop at the house of moon
And pause to relearn the wisdom of our fathers.[34]

We can understand that the politicians are a new tribe of their own creation in the new nations. They co-opt some professionals to join them but they are rejected by other sectors of the society as purveyors of modernity, since their progress is achieved at the expense of the general populace. The other sectors acquiesce to them, but this acquiescence is preached against by *all* the African writers. Achebe, through his character Odili, puts it best in explaining the *coup* and the peoples' reaction to the fall of the government. He muses:

> 'Koko had taken enough for the owner to see', said my father to me. . . . My father's words struck me because they were the very same words the villagers of Anata had spoken of Josiah, the abominated trader. Only in their case the words had meaning. The owner was the village and the village had a mind; it could say no to sacrilege. But in the affairs of the nation there was no owner, the laws of the village became powerless. Max was avenged not by the peoples' collective will but by one solitary woman who loved him. Had his spirit waited for the people to demand redress it would have been waiting still, in the rain and out in the sun, But he was lucky . . . [because he] inspired someone to come forward and shoot [his] murderer in the chest – asking to be paid.[35]

Hope for the future, therefore, seems in the works of the African writers to be with the people acting as individualists and led by the intellectuals, professionals and bureaucrats. However, no writer tells us how they are to win in the struggle for power against the politicians.

6 The Role of Women

The most memorable women in African literature, written largely by men, are the city types with fairly loose morals. Rubadiri describes them in a typical surrounding,

> In a corner of the room were 'girls'. Heavy makeup gave them a neutral expression. A mask that made them symbols of the new womanhood. The Astronaut made every woman significant. It gave every girl a sex symbol. Behind their masks they looked interesting, exciting and at the same time disgusting.[1]

That women must first have sexual emancipation before they can begin to function in a 'modern' social system, is clearly implied in the writings.

Consider the characters Simi and Jagua Nana. Simi is described in Soyinka's *The Interpreters*.

> Even children knew Simi. Wives knelt and prayed that their men might sin a hundred times with a hundred women, but their erring feet never lead them to Simi of the slow eyelids. For then men lost hope of salvation, their homes and children became ghosts of a past illusion, learning from Simi a new way of life, and love, immersed in cannibal's reality. . . . Simi broke men and friendships. . . . In company Simi would sit motionless, calm unacknowledging, indifferent to a host of admiring men. And yet she noticed them, and when they had gone, bluster emptied, pocket drained, manhood disgraced – for Simi matched them glass for glass and kept her mystery while the men were hollowed out and led out flabby or raucous, sadder but not wiser – then would Simi make her choice, her frozen eyelids betraying nothing. . . . Those who boasted that Simi gave them her love, that she lived for them, could never get the world to accept it, for Simi was cast in the

mould of distance and it made her innocent. As if there never
had been contact between her and the world, and these men
with whom she slept experienced nothing but desperation,
for they must see afterwards that they had never touched her.
To recapture the act was, in the glare of Simi's cold liver
gaze, a sacrilege. And so men could not tire of her whom they
never possessed and the illusion maddened them, began a
craving they could never end. . . . The men came and left
chastened. Big business, law, and the doctors were the most
confident of all, for at that time this was the prime profession,
the sign of the white man's talents. But Simi remained the
thorn-bush at night, and the glow worms flew fitfully around
and burnt out at her feet. . . . Hangers-on too, the many she
tolerated because they were protection. They ran her errands
of tact, invented her whims, took commissions for 'a good
word to your sister' and drank from the overflow of eternal
hope.[2]

Thus Simi is not only independent of men, but men are depen-
dent on her. They serve her. This is an inversion of what is generally assumed about the role of women in African society.
However, one must note that Simi dominates not only the men
but also her entire surroundings – the whole of life around her.
It is interesting to note that she ultimately picks up Egbo, the
fiery nationalist aristocrat as her permanent lover, but he is
stolen from her by a young, innocent and not so gracious college
co-ed.[3] Perhaps the writer is trying to convey two themes, one of
which is the independence of the free woman who can dominate
men in all settings. On the other hand Simi, as the free woman,
is in turn dominated by a young man, Agbo, and by the name-
less girl whose virtues are nationalism and commitment to
change through the acquisition of education.

Jagua Nana is a more interesting character if, for nothing
else, because we know her origin. She is the daughter of a catechist, that is to say one who has been converted to Christianity
but whom the missionaries dare not make a full pastor.[4] Her
father dotes on her and would like her to marry a filling-station
attendant who, by the father's standards, is really advanced.
Jagua Nana marries him, but unfortunately, she does not have
any children. To the extent that '. . . people in the country
believed that children were the most important things in the

world . . . [and] said every man and woman must have as many children as they could. . . .'[5] she is a failure, and therefore becomes a pariah when the husband takes a second wife. She seeks a new life in the city where she is first kept by a cheap African bandleader. Later she is procured by African houseboys for their employer – a white expatriate. He leaves her after his tour of duty and she goes into the clothing business, travelling outside the country to acquire materials and the 'Jagwaring' skills. Once her status is established through the success of her business Jagua – incidentally the name represents Jaguar, one of the most prestigious English sports cars – mixes in politics with Uncle Taiwo, a corrupt politician, to secure revenge against Freddie Namme, a young lawyer whom she had hoped to send to England as her future old-age insurance before he decided to do it on his own with the help of his wife, an African foreigner. Jagua Nana plays a crucial role in manipulating the votes of women for Uncle Taiwo. She also plays an important part in bringing two warring villages together by seducing one of the Chiefs and exacting the peace settlement as payment! She in short operates in whatever social system she finds herself.[6] Although she is unorthodox, her manipulation of all sorts of people, across all sorts of territorial boundaries and cultural and socio-economic classes, makes her a force to contend with. In a way she contrasts starkly with Simi in *The Interpreters*, but the dominant social idea exemplified by both is the independence and freedom of women. Because of them, other women can participate in politics, in fashions, and even to some extent in the running of their families and the State. In short, the Simis and Jaguas make it possible for women to become involved in public life.

One of the most intriguing women in African literature is Lawino. She has been described by Okot p'Bitek in *Song of Lawino – A Lament*. Although p'Bitek has taken a traditional Acoli form, the praise song, and written an extended poem about Lawino's husband Ocol, who is modern, the poem is not traditional since it is set in the present. Lawino criticises the modernity of Ocol, and of his attitude towards Black people she states,

> My husband pours scorn
> On Black people

.   .   .   .

> He says Black people are primitive
> And their ways are utterly harmful
> Their dances are mortal sins
> They are ignorant, poor and diseased.[7]

Here a woman criticises the arrogant educated who isolate themselves from their families who have not been as fortunate as they. By criticising the individual's movement away from the family she is upholding the values of the extended family, too.

Lawino has a lot to say about the modern woman, in this case her husband's new and modern wife,

> Brother when you see Clementine
> The beautiful one aspires
> To look like a white woman.
>
> Her lips are red hot
> Like glowing charcoal,
> She resembles the wild cat
> That has dipped its mouth in blood,
> Her mouth is like raw yaws
> It looks like an open ulcer,
> Like the mouth of a fiend!
> Tina dusts powder on her face
> And it looks so pale;
> She resembles the wizard
> Getting ready for the midnight dance
>
> She dusts the ash-dirt all over her face
> And when little sweat
> Begins to appear on her body
> She looks like a guinea fowl.[8]

Thus notions of beauty held in the West are rejected, and traditional concepts are re-emphasised. Lawino says,

> Listen Ocol, my old friend
> The ways of our ancestors
> Are good,
> Their customs are solid
> And not hollow
> They are not thin, not easily breakable

They cannot be blown away
By the winds
Because their roots reach deep in the soil

I do not understand
The ways of foreigners
But I do not despise their customs
Why should you despise yours?[9]

Lawino is not simply a throw back to a pre-colonial era advocating a return to the ways of the past. Rather she is a sensitive person who argues for cultural relativity and the acceptance of the validity of this position by those who call themselves educated and therefore modern, but who do nothing more than engage in blind imitation not necessarily of what is European but of what they perceive as European – such as the wearing of 'blanket suits', i.e., woollen suits in the middle of the hot season in Africa. These people ignore their traditional games,[10] dress,[11] methods of birth control,[12] dances,[13] and religion.[14] Lawino condemns the missionaries who only wanted to make her a house-girl,[15] and who babbled incoherent nonsense like,

Maria the Clean Woman
Mother of the hunchback
Pray for us
Who spoil things
Full of graciya[16]

She further condemns the missionaries and the educated as well because they cannot explain Christianity and show how the 'sacrifice' of Christ, for example, is any different from traditional sacrifices.[17]

Lawino comments on the stupidity of political parties and personalities in public life who say they essentially want the same things but cannot even agree to be seen together, and on the splitting of society, family and marriages because of political parties.[18] She gives this bitter comment on the political process,

And while those inside [government]
Eat thick honey
And ghee and butter
Those in the countryside

Die with the smell,
They re-eat the bones
That were thrown away
For the dogs

.   .   .   .

And when they [politicians] have
Fallen into things
They become rare,

.   .   .   .

They hibernate and stay away,
And eat!
They return to the countryside
For the next elections
Ocol says
They want Uhuru,
His brother says
They want Uhuru and Peace,
Both of them say
They fight ignorance and disease!

Then why do they not join hands
Why do they split up the army
Into two hostile groups?

.   .   .   .

. . . while the pythons of sickness
Swallow the children
And the buffaloes of poverty
Knock the people down
And ignorance stands there
Like an elephant.[19]

This is probably the most serious social critique by an African woman to be found in African literature. p'Bitek has not just written a powerful commentary on contemporary African life. To put these words into the mouth of a woman who is supposedly a traditionalist is to stress the point that women have a serious social responsibility to criticise and participate in the social order.

Through Lawino p'Bitek voices another of the concerns of many African writers, namely the fact that those Africans who were educated under British rule are now the ones who are most alienated from their tradition. Thus in the period of independence and during the quest for cultural identity in terms of the nation and the continent, the educated are the ones who really have no culture or tradition to fall back on. Lawino says to her husband,

> [You] may not know this
> You may not feel so
> But you behave like
> A dog of the white man!
>
> .   .   .   .   .   .
>
> The dogs of white men
> Are well trained
> And they understand English
>
> .   .   .   .   .   .
>
> . . . All our young men
> Were finished in the forest,
> Their manhood was finished
> In the classrooms,
> Their testicles
> Were smashed
> With large books.[20]

There is a paradox in this fact that the educated are the ones most alienated from traditional values. It is assumed in Western circles that most African societies aspire to be like the West. But in the African context there are a number of writers, p'Bitek among them, who raise the possibility that perhaps this is not such a desirable idea. To raise this question in the form of a lament by a woman who is supposedly a traditionalist is to give it very high potency indeed.

African women writers are relatively rare, as are powerful women characters in African literature. They may be a reflection of traditional values such as those expressed by the catechist in telling his life story. Of girls he states 'I will not bother much about for they did not interest me.'[21] In such a situation women would obviously not have been educated. In all African writing there is evidence that where schooling was possible, it was mainly for boys.

One female novelist, Flora Nwapa, has written a story in which the central character is a woman. Her name and the title of the book is *Efuru*. Efuru defies tradition by running away to get married without bride wealth. She rebels against doing farm work and against staying indoors the customary three months after circumcision. Believing she is barren she begins to engage in trade after her husband Adzua, like his father, becomes a vagabond. Ultimately Efuru returns to her father and marries one Gilbert, properly, that is to say, with bride price. However, they soon part because Gilbert, while on a trading journey, is put in jail and cannot attend her father's funeral – a serious taboo. Because in her travels Efuru has learned something about hospitals she takes the role of innovator in convincing a friend to go to the 'white man's' hospital for an operation on his reproductive organs, no mean act in past times!

Efuru is not a very strong character. Although the writer tries to present her as challenging some of the traditional ideas concerning the role of women, most of these battles are lost. After rejecting bride price once Efuru accepts it the second time. Her second marriage, however, is not really traditional. To play the trader role is to be innovative – this is non-traditional. Yet Efuru still feels bound to such an extent by the taboos surrounding burial of a parent that she renounces her second husband. Flora Nwapa probably set out to rehabilitate women in African literature but actually she seems to have failed since her major character is indecisive. The writer tells us that at one point Efuru was resigned to the fact that she could not have children and that she

> . . . dreamt of the woman of the lake, her beauty, her long hair and her riches. She had lived for ages at the bottom of the lake. She was old as the lake itself. She was happy. She was wealthy. She was beautiful. She gave women beauty and wealth but she had no child. She had never experienced the joy of motherhood. Why did the women worship her?[22]

Thus she suggests that the only way Efuru as a woman is freed is in achieving psychic peace in spite of the fact that she does not have children. This holds out hope for African women who are childless and who have been looked upon as outcasts by society.

This is the same kind of psychic peace arrived at by Chiaku, the widow in John Munoye's *The Only Son*. When her husband dies his relatives squander his wealth, in spite of injunctions by the husband before his death that the money is to be used to educate his son.[23] Chiaku is destitute but continues to work and beg until her son goes to school. In Cyprian Ekwensi's novel *Iska*, Remi, a modern girl in town, finds peace in her arrogant conviction that 'Men are inferior beings. Once they see you are different they are afraid. They cannot even get an erection because of fear.'[24]

Most of the modern women appearing in the literature are free from the bondage of traditional marriage mores. But in Remi's view this is not an unmixed blessing. She says,

> In modern Africa marriage is no longer easy. The control by the elders, the control by taboos and society, all have been lifted. Young couples are looking for roots. There are none. So what do they do? I don't think I shall marry. The more I think of it the surer I am. I do not think I shall ever marry. It is too difficult.[25]

Thus we see the burden of freedom overwhelming the free woman. Another woman in such a situation is Alice in Asare Konadu's *Shadow of Wealth*. She is only a simple villager 'acquired' by the director of a public corporation so as to be lavished with jewelery and clothes as the show piece of an important man! She is free from tradition, but she wonders – is this freedom?[26]

There are modern professional women in African literature who are free from traditions in a more wholesome way. However, they run into problems of generational conflict with their families. Consider Dehinwa in Soyinka's *The Interpreters*. She is fully accepted in the company of the interpreters, Sagoe, Egbo, Sekoni, Bandele and Lasunwon – her fellow professionals. What they do, she does. She is engaged to Sagoe who is not of her tribe. When her mother comes to see her, finds Sagoe with her, and objects, the following exchange takes place:

'Who I move with is my business.'

'Oh no it isn't your own business, and you don't go with who you like, not if you are my daughter. I should think I have a say in the matter. I haven't worked and slaved to send you to England and pulled strings to get you a really good position in the Senior Civil Service only to have you give me a Hausa grandson . . .'

'Alright, mama, alright. I am saving as fast as I can. I'll pay you back what you spent on me before I get married.'[27]

Although her mother relents after having said all this to her, Dehinwa would probably have remained with Sagoe anyway. With him she visits night clubs and attends seminars and recitals. She is an equal in the eyes of her future husband and his colleagues.

Central to modernity is the theme of alienation. This is the fate of Elizabeth, the main character of a short story by the same title by Grace Ogot. Elizabeth is a qualified, efficient secretary engaged to be married to a student whom she has left in the United States. She had returned home without marrying him because she wanted to marry within her people. She drifts from job to job because the men who employ her make sexual relationships a condition for her continuing to work. Ultimately one, Mr Jimbo, seduces and impregnates her. She has no choice but to commit suicide.[28] Another literary character is Filia Enu who is Ibo and engaged to be married to a Hausa. She loses her father and her husband, the latter in an Ibo–Hausa youth fight. Her mother meanwhile is collecting bride price in Iboland from an unsophisticated politician. Filia finally drifts into city life.[29]

Consider also the daughter of Durodayo who is married to a judge. Her father would like her to try to sway her husband into giving a lenient hearing to his friend. She points out to him that her husband, the 'incorruptible' judge, would not stand for that kind of interference in his legal duties. Because as a woman she is not supposed to oppose her father, the latter curses her.[30] Another interesting case is the story, *The Truly Married Woman*, by Abioseh Nicol. A woman lives by common law marriage with her husband for twelve years. When she is ultimately married after payment of bride price she refuses to rise and make tea for her husband in the morning. He raves and rants but she tells him '. . . for twelve years I have got up every morning at five to make tea for you and breakfast. Now I am a truly married woman [and] you must treat me with a little more respect. You are now my husband and not a lover. Get up and make yourself a cup of tea.'[31] This woman has found a new life in marriage and marriage is not bondage to her!

Other writers depict the roles of women in the past in various ways. James Ngugi explains to us why in general women have not had ownership rights historically. He writes

> . . . Long ago women used to rule this land and its men. They were harsh and men began to resent their hard hand. So when all the women were pregnant, men came together and overthrew them. Before this women owned everything. . . . It was then Waiyaki understood why his mother owned nothing.[32]

Grace Ogot in the novel *The Promised Land* tells us of Ochola and his wife Nyapol. Ochola wants to move from a densely populated area to one that is less crowded and has better farming land which, however, does not belong to their tribe. Nyapol is reluctant. When they ultimately go and the husband falls sick it is Nyapol who vehemently advocates returning to the tribal lands even though it means losing all their wealth.[33]

Achebe in *Things Fall Apart* depicts Anasi, first wife of Nwakibie, as accepting her role as 'subordinate' to her husband.

> Anasi was the first wife and the others could not drink before her, so they stood waiting. . . . She walked up to her husband and accepted the horn from him. She went down on one knee, drank a little and handed back the horn. She rose, called him by his name and went back to her hut. The other wives drank in the same way, in the proper order, and went away. . . . The men then continued their drinking and talking.[34]

However, as the literature reveals, although the idea of women addressing their husbands as 'my lord', 'please do so my lord,' 'I am sorry my lord',[35] may have been part of traditional society, it is no longer the expected and accepted rule.

Soyinka's play *A Dance of the Forest* concerns the role of the female ancestor. The play hinges on the return of the dead to life and how they are received by the living. Among the living is Madam Tortoise – Rola. When the dead woman calls on her, claiming she is a relative Rola tells her

> Get out and pack your things. Think of it. Think of it yourself. What did she think I was? I can't take anyone who happens to wander in, just because she claims to be my auntie.

My Auntie! . . . This whole family business sickens me. Let everybody lead their own lives.[36]

Rola is a prostitute and she just wants room to entertain! In fact in the past she was a 'prostitute queen' in the court of Mata Kharibu,[37] and the woman who has returned and whom she rejects in the name of her individualism and personal rights vis-à-vis the family, is her own spirit from the 'ancestor' period. Thus Soyinka shows us a contradiction in ancestor praise. Some ancestors are not worthy of worship and acceptance, but rejection of them in the name of breaking with tradition can be risky.

The more significant fact is that Madam Tortoise, Rola, appears in the past and in the present as a prostitute, pointing out that women liberated from the hold of tradition are usually found in marginal professions and not as simple housewives, a point made earlier with regard to Simi and Jagua Nana. Perhaps this is an anti-feminist bias in African writing. The bias is not confined to men writers but is found also among women writers like Grace Ogot and Barbara Kimenye.[38]

There are writers who depict women in purely political roles. One such writer is Gabriel Okara in *The Voice*. Okolo, the central character, who is looking for justice and truth in society, is imprisoned because of his criticism of the governing officials and their corruption in acquiring money, cars and concrete buildings. He is saved by an old illiterate woman who in her wisdom sees his worth with regard to society.[39] Another political role for women is to be found in Wole Soyinka's play, *Kongi's Harvest*. Segi, who at one time was Kongi's mistress, rebels against totalitarianism and organises the prostitutes into a Woman's Auxiliary Corps. They pretend to be loyal to Kongi, but since 'They all have husbands, sons and brothers rotting in forgotten places'[40] they really intend to overthrow him. The opportunity comes when Kongi executes Segi's father on the day of the harvest festival when Kongi expects to consolidate total spiritual and temporal power in himself. This is to be achieved by eating a yam consecrated and offered to him rather than to the gods by the spiritual leader Danlola. The Woman's Auxiliary Corps is supposed to cook the yam, but instead they offer Kongi the head of Segi's father.[41] This breaks the spell and the hold of Kongi on the population. Thus an ex-mistress leading a brigade of ex-prostitutes saves the society from a despot.

Another direct political role for a woman is found in Aubrey Kachingwe's *No Easy Task*. Here a madam, Sleepy Aunt, who is illiterate, is the financial backer of the nationalist movement.[42] A similar but negative emancipated role is the one played by Aunt Bimp who charms her way to the hearts of the politicians who handle government contracts and then goes into the construction business. She is part of the corruption. She knows nothing about cement and sand but the corruption of the system has served to liberate her.[43]

One of the most heroic women in African literature is Eunice in Achebe's *A Man of the People*. She is a lawyer. Her fiance, Max, is a lawyer too. They, together with other professionals, found a party to fight the corruption of the independence government. They battle the established party seriously. On the day of the election Max and Eunice go to investigate the stuffing of ballot boxes by women who, following the example and instructions of Mrs Koko, have secreted extra ballots in their bosoms. Max is run over by a jeep hired to do so by Chief Koko, just outside the voting booths.

> Eunice had been missed by a few inches when Max had been felled. She stood like a stone figure . . . for some minutes more. Then she opened her handbag as if to take out a handkerchief, took out a pistol instead and fired two bullets into Chief Koko's chest. Only then did she fall down on Max's body and begin to weep like a woman; and then the policeman seized her and dragged her away. A very strange girl, people said.[44]

After this the rival gangs of Max and Chief Koko fight it out, all across the nation. The Prime Minister reappoints the former cabinet, with Mrs Koko as Minister of Women's Affairs. She is appointed as a measure to quiet the market women's guild, but the government falls anyway and the army takes over. The army declares Max the hero of the revolution and releases Eunice.[45] Thus the credit for the revolution goes to Eunice since she catalysed the reaction. She is commendable in having the will to avenge not only Max but what he stood for. This is a free woman with not only a sense of individual responsibility but social conscience as well.

Any discussion of the role of women is incomplete without a consideration of polygamy. Polygamy, as a form of the institution of marriage, '. . . was too serious a thing to be entered into on the whim of a young couple. It was a contract to be made, after earnest consideration and long discussion between the families. . . .'[46] Although African writers depict modern women as alienated, as prostitutes or as political activists, they usually reject the view that polygamy is a value to be propagated. They point out, however, that we should accept it as a valid norm in eras past. Thus the polygamous families are depicted in history as having been suitable for that period.

The central character in Egbuna's novel, *Wind Versus Polygamy*, is the traditional Chief Ozuomba who is being tried by an *independent* African government which has just passed non-retroactive legislation abolishing polygamy. Ozuomba sees this as enforcement of foreign culture, to wit

> I, an African Paramount Chief, am being committed to trial today because I refuse to conform with the European conception of ideal marriage. I am in chains today because I believe that the freedom we fought for was the freedom to live our own life our own way, our African way and not the license to take over the bleaching of the African personality where the oppressor left off. I am brought before this court for not subscribing to the creed that every mistake in Europe must be an accepted canon in Africa.[47]

Ozuomba sees polygamy as the natural way.

> Wholesale monogamy is the wrong foundation for durable marriage in any society. Marriage failures over there indicate the rebellion of man against the trammels of unnatural conventions. Man wants to be natural. To be polygamous is natural. It is living life to the full.[48]

The basis for polygamy, Ozuomba argues, is the biogenic superiority of man's reproductive capacity and the inferiority of women's biogenic reproductive capacity.

> . . . An average man is capable of having three thousand children in his lifetime. But the lifetime capacity of the average

woman is ten only. In other words, man has got what we call abundant talent. Surely he must share this talent with his sisters according to his ability, and distribution among women according to their needs. Sex democracy must prevail.[49]

Beyond this there is also the question of the absolute numbers of the species.

On the other hand . . . woman has a numerical superiority over men. In fact, throughout the animal kingdom, the female species always outnumber the males. The difference is even intensified in mankind by wars. The position therefore is this. Man enjoys potential superiority and suffers numerical inferiority. Woman enjoys numerical superiority and suffers potential inferiority. . . . The problem which therefore confronts society is nothing more than fair distribution. The only rational distribution is polygamy. . . . If society insists on tying one man to one woman in spite of the numerical disparity I just mentioned, the question is what becomes of those excess women. . . . To make a woman to be unwillingly barren is the worst type of sentence that can be passed on her. . . . Fools have been heard to say that polygamy is the slavery of women. In actuality, it is her emancipation.[50]

The chief evil of monogamy, Ozuomba continues, is

. . . lack of consideration for the sick, the deformed, the blind, the maimed. Millions of women in the world today are doomed to perpetual spinsterhood just because they have these purely physical misfortunes. They are born only to die again, and in between, to decay in telling isolation in homes.[51]

Monogamy is also the chief cause of prostitution.

Prostitution is the principle estuary of that sea of social maladjustment of which monogamy is the only source. First you have an overflow of women who are not married and who will not marry and yet they have biological assignments to fulfil. Secondly, you have wretched married men who want an outlet from their monogamous insularity. Thirdly, you have a regiment of terrified bachelors who prefer their freedom to the imprisonment of monogamy. Put all three together in one community and the result is a rich

manure in which prostitution germinates in glorious profu-
sion.[52]

Finally, Ozuomba justifies polygamy in terms of the social-
isation process which leads children to accept outsiders.

> It has been proved . . . that children brought up in polyga-
> mous establishments are much more sociable than their
> counterparts from monogamous homes. . . . In polygamous
> homes, children are conditioned to accept the differences in
> various aspects of life as natural. . . . Make polygamy univer-
> sal in the world today and hate, clan–complex and racialism
> are for ever guillotined.[53]

Of course we expect a mind such as Ozuomba's to deny the
equality of the sexes, but it is ironic to hear him argue that
women must be sexually controlled! This is similar to Aluko's
argument that 'White man has only one wife. . . . When he
made the rule one man to one wife, he was trying to avoid
woman trouble'.[54] Not necessarily because of humanity or
notions of equality of women! Ozuomba makes the two points
in the following manner.

> There is no such things as the equality of the sexes. Either
> man stays on top and plays man. Or woman stays on top and
> dictates to man. The woman is more ruthless when she has
> the least opportunity of power. In the West she created the
> myth of gentlemanliness to achieve her purpose. . . . And in
> the East, the woman wields her power in the dark. She has
> created the illusion that she is weak and humble and frail.
> She does not even clamour for equality. . . . She is more cun-
> ning than her counterpart in the West in this respect because
> she gets her way without friction which an open declaration
> of war for equality makes inevitable. . . . Women are the
> arch-enemy of men and we must control them sexually. Poly-
> gamy is the most legitimate armoury for this operation. . . .
> Because sex is an agent of control in nature.[55]

This then is the most extreme argument for polygamy. We
should note that it is put in the mouth of a traditionalist and not
a modern individual, so it thereby loses much of its relevance to
the new social systems even though it addresses itself to the
present and does so in the logic of the present. Above all, the

argument is unrepresentative of African writing since most of the literature shows women and men mainly in non-polygamous settings.

A novel which deals with polygamy in a much less dogmatic fashion but offers instead a sympathetic portrayal of the traditional role of women and how they perceived themselves in a polygamous society is Ounora Nzekwu's *Highlife for Lizards*. Agom is married to Udezue who is a farmer. For a period of about eight years she is unable to have children. This puts such a strain on their relationship, because both are laughed at, that they begin to fight. Udezue recollects,

> All the girls who were married at about the same time as his wife were pregnant, but Agom was not. Their babies came one after another. Still Agom was far from pregnant. Her inability to keep abreast with her compatriots filled her with disappointment and shame. She hid herself in the house most of the time and public appearances when she could not avoid them proved an ordeal for her. Then he heard the taunts of his friends and the sarcastic remarks of his enemies about pouring his manhood, and his own voice as he laughed it off and reminded them that early marriages did not always spell early procreation. Next he heard the bickerings of his relations – expressions of their concern which were later turned into contempt – who pointed out that though he was a young man, he was not growing stronger, and persuaded him to take a new wife. There was no advantage to be doting over a sterile woman.[56]

Udezue takes a second wife, Nwandi, who was a childhood friend of Agom's. The 'taking' of this second wife is interesting as a social idea. Nwandi is already married in another polygamous family and all she does is walk out of her former husband's home and go to Udezue's. Since she is not intercepted on the way, once she arrives and Udezue acknowledges her presence, nothing can happen to her. Thus women were not enslaved as such, since they could pick up and go at any time,[57] thereby dissolving their marriage. Agom, who in the meantime has gone into trading (substantiating, incidentally, our hypothesis that the innovator in African literature is always portrayed as alienated from traditional values) does not approve of

Nwandi as a second wife. Nwandi is lazy and although she provides the family with a female child she is insecure and wants to drive a wedge between Agom and Udezue. Her plan is to give birth to a boy, in that way confirming her superiority as a woman and mother of the first son. In pursuit of this goal she runs around with medicine-men and other men who are more potent than Udezue. This leads to her being thrown out of the marriage, leaving her little girl behind.[58]

Agom conceives. She too expects a boy.

> For a boy would bring her greater recognition among her husband's kinsmen Besides a boy would qualify her for burial among them when she died. This would be a fitting end to her long life of toil in Ojele where she fancied she now belonged but was not qualified to belong. It required more than residence over a long period to win that honour. Until she had a baby boy her corpse would be carried home and buried among her own people who would willingly take her back for she was their own. But the strong feeling that the ties binding her to her people had weakened considerably with her long absence from among them generated the fear that she would not rest peacefully in death, among a people from whom she was so much detached in real life. That fear made a baby boy more preferable.[59]

Agom does bear a son, out in the fields, and he barely survives the exposure. Now her social status is assured, so much so that she becomes the leader of a group of women who are refusing to buy water from the government,[60] and thrives as a trader during the process. She has other children. Then Agom does what is most crucial with respect to the role of women. She asks her husband to take another wife.

> Agom's second baby, a girl called Chinedo (God mends), came two years and three months after Onyema, her first child, was born. Right from the day she became pregnant her conscience pricked her. By local standards the baby had come nine months too soon and was, for peopl, a genuine proof of her sexual laxity. . . .
>
> Agom was a very practical woman. She admitted herself the possibility of this situation recurring in the future and

began to think of steps to prevent it.[61]

We see that the reason Agom urges her husband to take a second wife is based on a principle of birth-control. If children are spaced three years apart not only will they be fewer but also the woman will stay healthier. She tells Udezue that

> . . . she was not getting younger and stronger; . . . she needed spacing out her pregnancies. That way she would live longer, share in mother's joy of watching her children grow and get married and have children of their own, and Udezue would have her for some more years.[62]

It is not easy to convince Udezue that he should marry a second wife. His desire seems to have been only for children. Now that he has three, one Nwandi's and two Agom's, he is satisfied. But Agom insists. (I quote extensively.)

> 'I think it is time you thought seriously about getting yourself another wife,' she said.
>
> 'I remember I once told you I didn't want another wife,' he answered.
>
> 'Of course you did, But things are different now from what they were then!'
>
> 'Are they? Do you think I have forgotten my experiences with Nwandi?'
>
> 'You brought the embers that burnt you. You knew what stock she came from and yet, you fell for her.'
>
> 'Well I don't want another woman in this house!'
>
> 'I'm sure you've not given it adequate thought yet,' she said coolly. 'You always lament the absence of children in the family. How many more children do you think I can give you? You know I am getting older and weaker and as a result I need to space out my pregnancies more than I've done; otherwise we'd be inviting death.'
>
> Udezue did not answer.
>
> 'I realize Nwadi has frightened you,' she went on. 'But that experience should not scare you away from doing what you yourself know is right.'
>
> 'Well this is a bad season to start thinking about marriage,' Udezue said after a long silence. 'The farm work has eaten up all my money.'

'Let that not worry you. If only you'll agree to taking another wife, I'll run the marriage expenses for you.

Udezue thought over this offer for a long time. At last he said, 'All right, I agree. But who is the bride?'

'I'm leaving the choice to you,' she said.

'No,' he said quickly. 'I tried once before and it failed. This time I'll leave it to you.'

Hesitatingly, Agom said, 'Have you ever thought Ugoye would make a decent wife?'

'Ugoye?' Udezue did not believe his ears. He said the name with the feeling of repugnance colouring his voice. 'That little cockroach?' he added and roared with laughter.

He had expressed his dislike for the dirty, ill-mannered, fragile girl that Ugoye was when she first came (as a household servant), by referring to her as a 'little cockroach.' But he had refrained from interfering with her continued stay in the house because she was not his direct responsibility. With time he had come to accept her as part of the household and though he could vouch for her industry, honesty and her other virtues, he remained blind to her growth, her physical charm, and continued in moments of annoyance to refer to her or even address her as the 'little cockroach.'

'You know,' Agom said smoothly, 'that she is a virtuous girl from a good family. She's been with us for almost three years and I've watched her every step in all that period. I'm convinced she'll make a good wife. Besides, she's fully grown and has charm and pleasing disposition. She loves children too, and she adores you.'

'Ugoye?' he repeated distantly.

'What's wrong with her?' Agom asked. . . .

'I'll think it over,' he said without enthusiasm and lay down on the bed with a deep sigh.

Agom left him and went into her room satisfied that she had shaken his conviction about not wanting another wife but afraid that he might not approve of Ugoye. She was still in her room when Udezue went into the kitchen. Sitting on the low wall of the kitchen he began to study Ugoye who was absorbed in her task of hewing firewood in the back yard. He was so absorbed in the exercise that he did not know when Agom came and stood behind him and for a moment watched him concentrate on the elegant figure that was swinging her axe in carefree abandon.

'Well?' she said softly.

He came to with a start and smiled indulgently. 'I'm seeing her with new eyes,' he said. His eyes travelled up to Agom's face and down again before setting once more on the girl. 'I suppose she's as good as any other spinster in town.'

'What does that mean?'

'Unless you've got someone else in your mind, I think she'll do,' he said. 'Anyway, since you're paying the bill the decision is entirely yours.'

'I'll go and see her parents tomorrow.'[63]

The purpose of this rather extended quotation is to illustrate the role played by the woman in choosing another wife for her husband. Although the quotation may be said to illustrate a weak husband, this is clearly not so as the rest of the book testifies. He runs his home but his wife's role is clear. She can make choices which are fundamental in the structuring of the home and, by linkages, also the society. Agom speaks with Ugoye's parents, who consent, and she is married to Udezue.

The resultant change in Ugoye's status from step-daughter, ward or servant to wife in the same household did not in fact alter the relationship between her and Agom. She regarded Agom not as a co-wife, but as her benefactor and mistress. She treated her with the greatest respect and took her words as laws. She continued to look after the children and do the household duties when Agom was away.

On her part, Agom occasionally scolded her when she went wrong, but she never talked down to her. She guided her along the path of her new life and kept her happy with presents of clothes and trinkets. The following year Ugoye had a baby boy and the year after Agom brought forth her third child, a girl, whom they called Ndidi – patience is the strength of the soul.[64]

Thus the idea of polygamy in a structured society is not as anti-individualistic as some would have us believe. There are areas where women can function as individuals, perhaps not as independently as under a monogamous setting, but with enough independence for their own psychic health.

Agom, on being told by a modern girl that the inequality of the role of women in a polygamous setting vis-à-vis the role of men gives men power and influence at the expense of women, disagrees,

> 'The creator is no fool,' Udezue remarked with an air of wisdom. 'There can only be one helmsman to guide a canoe. Any canoe that tries having two will end in the deep.'
>
> 'But think again, my daughters,' Agom said sweetly and Udezue watched out for mischief. 'Who really wields the power and exerts all the influence? Is it man who by virtue of natural laws has an edge over woman or is it woman, man's best confidant and natural adviser?'[65]

The point is not lost on her husband, who storms out!

We see that African writers view polygamy as having been valuable in the past but they point out that it is incompatible with the demands of modern life. However, they make it clear in the literature that women can function as individuals in today's society more easily in the towns than in the rural and therefore traditional areas. The most liberated women in the towns are not presented as the most admirable in terms of moral values. They are often prostitutes or mistresses. Career women seem to end with psychological and familial upsets and, many times, in suicide. On the other hand the wives of the new elites are usually presented as semi-traditionalist and therefore unsuited to the lives of their husbands, who look to the emancipated town women – be they career women or Jagua Nanas – for companionship in social-political life.

7 The Rural–Urban Contradiction

There is a tension in African writing concerning the relative roles of the city and the village in determining the relationship of individuals to the society. James Ene Henshaw points this out very clearly when he notes that the city-dweller Ewia Ekunyah has three major problems, his traditional wife, the need to win an election, and the need to gain access to the ranks of the elite. 'Whether to employ the methods dictated to him by his reason, education and religion to solve his domestic and public problems or to employ traditional methods, which in this case, are represented by a versatile medicine-man.'[1] The tension between the urban and rural sectors of the society does not stem from the geographical distinction alone. It stems more from the fact that the two situations call for radically different rules of operation in the particular milieu. One who is in an urban milieu finds it 'irksome to fit bed-rock traditionalism into his every day concept of a newer Africa. Unlike his forefathers,... "things fall apart" between him and tradition and now he is "no longer at ease" with the demands of the new European ways in which he finds himself.'[2]

The urbanite cannot afford the luxury of the life of a Danda, the major character of a novel similarly called, who lives in a traditional environment where even if he does not work he will have shelter, food and the chance to be merry all his life.[3] Yet when the urbanite acquires the trappings of Western man – a car, stone house, radiogram and woollen suits – his rural counterpart asks him '[Do] you think we of this community do not relish long cars to cruise in and places to live in.'[4] The rural African thereby directs his hostility toward the urbanite – hostility based on the aspiration of the rural people to have those

73

things found in and associated with the city. Because they are less in number, city dwellers are subject to question and, one might say, threatened by the rural population who are greater numerically and also to some extent more influential, since tradition is on their side.

The problem of value conflicts is portrayed by James Ngugi in *Weep Not Child*. He writes:

> The young men of the village usually allowed the elders to lead talks while they listened. But those others who came with Kori and Boro from the big city seemed to know a lot of things. They usually dominated the talks. And because most of them had been to the war they were able to compare the affairs of the land with the lands to which they had been. They did not joke and laugh as young men usually did, but their faces were grave, as they talked of the foreign lands, war, their country, the big unemployment and the stolen lands.[5]

Thus there was tension between the villagers and those who had been to the towns and the world outside their village. They had already become politically conscious in comparison with the village dwellers, and they could not accept the roles expected of them once they returned. They saw life in a different light. Above all they knew that what had been was not necessarily what had to be. They rejected the idea that the rural order was the only order possible. They advocated political agitation against the colonisers.

On the other hand, after independence the urban African is identified with the new order of things and is rejected by the rural population as a prostitution of something they have always had. This is the reaction of the villagers when Lombe, in Rubadiri's *No Bride Price*, comes home accused of bribery:

> The word had quietly gone round that Lombe was at his mother's house. Food began to arrive from the homes nearby. This was the custom. One welcomed strangers and especially relatives because they belonged. This thing that had fallen on Lombe's house had fallen on all of them. It was their duty to see it through and finalize it properly. This awe inspiring concern of man for man is what the big people in

the big new government in the big city had been trying to write down. They had given it a big name, 'African Socialism.' They had mixed it and patched it up with a lot of other big ideas from unknown countries. They had violently yoked it to all sorts of other ideas and called it 'Policy' and now Land-Rovers and loudspeakers with recorded music came each week to explain it to the people who lived in Lombe's village. They listened patiently to the young pioneers in their uniforms and party slogans. Children playing at toy soldiers explaining to them the wisdom of the old. The old women of the village had been made to dance to these young gods in praise of this thing called 'Socialism' – others called it 'Progressive Communalism'. Then the smart and strong and very powerful young children called the pioneers had demanded chickens, cards and organization and had left to report to Chozo [Lombe's corrupt Minister who is smearing him] their great success after beating up a number of old men and women who had not come to listen to their pantomime. Did they not know that if God on earth sends his little angels to spread the word, that everyone must come and listen? Food and more food came to Lombe's hut. . . . Much of this food was not going to be eaten by Lombe. Everyone knew this. He tasted as much as he could and sent it to the children waiting outside. They had a field day of eating. In this way they learned that strangers and relations coming back are important parts of their way of life.[6]

The city operates on a 'modern' system where organisation is the basis of power and prestige, where political organisations are used to effectuate control. This is what the village objects to because the old way is based not on organisation but on the structuring of roles. These roles are known. Part of the general knowledge is the belief that the young should not have much to say about the social system. When the young pioneers act, then, as the major purveyors of ideology or change there is consternation in the village, suggesting that the legitimacy of change which comes from the city is doubted.

From the point of view of the villagers, very 'peculiar' customs exist in the city. Ol' Man Forest-Emorwen, a character in Cyprian Ekwensi's *Beautiful Feathers*, who lives in the forest, offers the following critique of the city. 'Some say I am mad. Yes, I know they say it. But it is they who are mad because they cannot understand! They and their noisy towns. God made this village. But man made the towns; artificial things. When I go to Benin I run back to this place.'[7] To criticise the city as an artificial creation is to point out that the village accepts only natural creativity. That is to say, the village does not accept the notion that man in the image of God is a creator himself. In contrast to the city, where man seeks to shape nature and fate and therefore there is chance for advancement and development (that much-maligned word), in the village the acceptance is only of destiny.

It should be noted that sometimes rural Africa delegates one of its own to act as its 'eyes and ears' in the complex world of the city. That is why people like Obi Okwonkwo are sent to England by their village so that when they return the village can say, 'This is mine.'[8] The need to possess that which belongs to the village stems from the fact that strangers are tightly shut out from rural society. As Sunma tells us in *The Strong Breed*, a play by Soyinka, 'Even if [one] lived here [in a village] for a life time, [one] could remain a stranger.'[9] This rejection of strangers is coupled with the rejection of outside ideas or innovations because they are a threat to the existing order. There are even attempts to continue the hold of the village on its descendants in the city by use of village-based and sanctioned organisations like the Osa Descendants Union in Soyinka's *The Interpreters*, the Umuofia Progressive Union in Achebe's *No Longer At Ease* and the Ndigwe Patriotic Union in Clement Agunwa's *More Than Once*.[10] Such organisations try to perpetuate in the city what was and still is the mode of life in the village.

During the independence period they served as an important link with the nascent political parties.

Since the city is open to change and at the same time unstructured in terms of knowledge of what the individual is to do, we find that when grief comes to any character in the literature his refuge is the village. Lombe in *No Bride Price*[11] returns to the village after he is falsely accused of bribery. Similar action is taken by Ashoka in *When Love Whispers*,[12] by Wilson in *Beautiful Feathers*,[13] Jagua Nana in *Jagua Nana*,[14] and by many others. Such reactions are basically detrimental to change in the individuals, because they never become liberated enough to shape their own destiny. They can always fall back on the village for salvation. Thus it seems that for individuals to act and adjust to a 'modern' social system they have to be free agents and therefore open to individual catastrophe if it befalls them. What this ensures is individual rationality and hence some kind of collective rationality in the social system.

To illustrate the point, consider the following exchange between Jagua Nana and Dennis – a thief in the city. Jagua tells him

> 'Dennis, I wan' to tell you something.' Dis kind of life dat you follow, you think is a good life?'
>
> Dennis smiled. 'what you wan' me to do? To go an' be clerk? Awright! I already try go find work. Dem ask me to bring bribe-money. I give one man ten pound, and he chop de money and he no fin' work for me. How I go do? I mus' chop. Myself and de taxi-man who die, sometime we kin make one hundred pound by Saturday. Sometime, we don' see anythin'. But we live happy. I got my girl Sabina, and she love me well. . . . Me we pay our rent regular. We never look money de face, an' say "dis money is too much." We jus' spen' to get anythin' we want. Anythin'. So why worry? De day dat de policeman catch we, we go. Is all de same whedder we live in cell or outside de cell.'[15]

Dennis has learned to make choices and to shape his life. Although it may be conceded that he should perhaps be shaping it according to other values, that is a qualitative judgement. In an objective sense, Dennis is free from the totalitarianism of tradition, and that is a very important freedom not just for the sake of modernity but ultimately, one hopes, for the sake of democracy. The same point is made in another part of the book when Ekwensi tells us that

> Jagua felt caught up in the unbelievable atmosphere of trickery, opportunism, intuition, daring and amazing decisions. People who lived here (in the city) she was sure, did not care what happened elsewhere, they were hard-headed and complete strangers to laziness.[16]

Of course the urban motive is to acquire money There may

be dissent on the wisdom of making this a major value, but it is a fact that it tends to dominate in modern urban social and political systems. The quest for money leads to new values. Jagua and Freddie find this out.

> Like Freddie [she] was an Ibo from Eastern Nigeria, but when she spoke to him she always used pidgin English, because living in Lagos City they did not want too many embarrassing reminders of clan or custom. They and many others were practically strangers in a town where all came to make fast money by faster means and greedily to seek positions that yielded even more money.[17]

Thus we are told as bluntly as possible that the city is a liberating agent from custom and tradition. It is a place for economic betterment, and above all it is a place for creation of new social systems – dominated by money. 'Brotherhood ends where money begins.'[18] All is sacrificed to the money god. Jagua says,

> The Syrian's money would buy her that new dress from Kingsway. She had already pictured herself in it. She loved Freddie well, but his whole salary could not buy that dress. He must understand that taking the money from the Syrian did not mean she loved him less. . . . He should know by now that in the Tropicana [a night club] money always claimed the first loyalty.[19]
>
> In a city where money was the idol of the women, an idol worshipped in every waking and sleeping moment, sentiment was a mere pastime.[20]

But money is not the only value stressed in the town. Often radical ideas about which groups should dominate in the society are also acquired and expressed in the most poignant ways. Remi, a modern professional girl in town who has learned about efficiency, uses it to restructure her understanding of the traditional male–female roles in the social system. She concludes, 'Men are inferior beings. Once they see you are efficient they are afraid. They cannot even get an erection because of fear.'[21] This woman, like Simi, Elizabeth, Dehinwa and Jagua, who were all discussed in the section on women, is free and no tradition or political system is going to

imprison her mind again. This is also true of Igwezu, a character in Wole Soyinka's *The Swamp Dwellers.* Igwezu and his
brother go to the city. When he returns home he is broke and
finds his crops destroyed by the flood. He says:

> When I went with harshness in the city, I did not complain.
> When I felt the nakedness of its hostility, I accepted it. . . .
> When I saw its knife sever the ties and the love of kinship and
> turn brother against brother . . .[22]

Asked what his brother did to him, he answers

> Nothing but what happens to a newcomer to the race. The
> city reared itself in the air, and with the strength of its legs of
> brass kicked the adventurer in the small of the back. . . . The
> wound heals quicker if it is left unopened. What took place is
> not worthy of memory . . . Does it not suffice that in the end I
> said to myself . . . I have a place, a home, and though it lies in
> the middle of the slough, I will go back to it. And I have a
> little plot of land which has rebelled against the waste that
> surrounds it, and yields a little fruit for the asking. I sowed
> this land before I went away. Now is the time for harvesting,
> and the cocoa-pods must be bursting with fullness . . . I came
> back to the village with consolation in my heart. I came back
> with the assurance of one who has lived with his land and
> tilled it faithfully. . . . It was never in my mind . . . the
> thought that the farm could betray me so totally, that it could
> drive the final wedge in this growing loss of touch.[23]

Asked by the Kadiye, the priest who offers the sacrifices to
the water god, why he is disillusioned Igwezu continues:

> I'm afraid I have had my turn already. I lost everything; my
> savings, even my standing as a man. I went into debt. . . . No,
> holy one. It was not my wife. But what I offered had a lot in
> common with her. I put down the harvest from my farm. . . .
> No. They are not fools; my brother least of all. He is anything
> but a fool.[24]

Igwezu believes that his crops were destroyed because the
Kadiye did not make the sacrifices. The Kadiye eats the sacrifices – that is why he is so fat. Igwezu frightens him by holding a
razor at his throat, and then adds 'Go quickly, Kadiye . . . And

next time that you wish to celebrate the stopping of the rains, do not choose a barber whose harvest rots beneath the mire, one who can read the lie in the fat of your eyes.'[25] Then he ends by stating to his bondsman, 'Only the children and the old stay here, bondsman. Only the innocent and dotards.'[26]

This rather extended quotation points out the new economic relationships which arise because of the peculiar tension between the city and the village. The brothers go to town. One becomes rich and the other fails. As a result the rich one, because of money, is able to steal the poor one's wife and also to get him into debt by loaning him money, using his crops as collateral. The village priest in spite of 'sacrifices' has failed to protect him. Thus Igwezu, through economic tragedy, is able to break the hold of the traditional religion and notions of fate. He walks away a free and independently acting individual. Because he condemns the village so vehemently we can assume that he goes back to the city to shape his life and not be held in bondage by fate. He rejects subsistence farming and existence in the same way as do the 'gaberdine boys', characters in Duodu's novel *The Gab Boys*, when they pour scorn on the idea of subsistence existence.[27]

Because the village has always provided a very secure framework, those who leave for the city seek ways to approximate this security. We have already pointed out the role of 'descendants unions'. Another very common method is the 'revival churches'. It is said that 'revival churches' were forms of protest prior to the nationalist movement proper. If this hypothesis holds perhaps it may be argued that they are also continuities of traditional forms. Given the urban–rural dichotomy, perhaps they are an adaptation of the 'Secret societies [which] were powerful instruments of government and social discipline.'[28] At any rate, the revival churches cater to the dissatisfied and the alienated. Listen to Brother Jero, one of its prophets.

> I am glad I got here before any customers – I mean worshippers – well, customers if you like. I always get that feeling every morning that I am a shopkeeper waiting for customers . . . strange, dissatisfied people. I know they are dissatisfied because I keep them dissatisfied. Once they are full they won't come again. Like my good apprentice, Brother

Chiume. He wants to beat his wife, but I won't let him. If I do he will become contented, and then that's another of my flock gone for ever. As long as he doesn't beat her, he comes here feeling helpless and so there is no chance of his rebelling against me.[29]

We can see more clearly the quest for security when Brother Chiume, a civil service messenger, prays,

> Tell our wives not to give us trouble. And give us money to have a happy home. Give us money to satisfy our daily necessities. Make you not forget those of us who struggle daily. Those who clerk today, make them Chief Clerk tomorrow. . . . Those who are petty trader today, make them big contractor tomorrow. Those who dey sweep street today, give them their own big office tomorrow. If we dey walka today, give us our own bicycle tomorrow. I say those who dey walka today, give them their own bicycle tomorrow. Those who have bicycle today, they will ride their own car tomorrow.[30]

Few of the intellectuals participate in or understand the role of these churches.[31] In Soyinka's novel *The Interpreters*, Sagoe sees one revival church meeting as contributing only to a sensational newspaper story. Kola sees the worshippers only as subjects for his painting. It is only Bandele who questions the rest of the group's cynicism concerning the story they are told that Noah, one of the revivalists, was pitch black, died, and was resurrected white. Bandele, asked later on whether he had believed the story, states

> It did not matter whether I did or not. But at least one thing was obvious, this man did go through some critical experience. If he has chosen to interpret it in a way that would bring some kind of meaning into peoples' lives, who are you to scoff at it?[32]

In the final analysis, the search for peace in the tension between the social systems of the city and the village can be summed up in the words of George Awoonor-Williams who writes in 'Exiles':

> The return is tedious
> And the exiled souls gathered at the beach

Arguing and deciding their future
Should they return home
And face the fences the termites had eaten
And see the dunghill that has mounted their birthplace?
. . . The final strokes will land them on forgotten shores,
They committed the impiety of self-deceit
Slashed, cut and wounded their souls
And left the mangled remainder in manacles. . . .

The moon, the moon is our father's spirit
At the stars entrance the night revellers gather
To sell their chatter and inhuman sweat to the gateman
And shuffle their feet in agonies of birth.
Lost souls, lost souls, lost souls that are
still at the gate.[33]

8 The Individual–Community Contradiction

> Could I, early sequester'd from my tribe
> Free a lead-tether'd scribe
> I should answer her communal call
> Lose myself in her warm caress
> Intervolving earth, sky and flesh.[1]

The above statement is by a modern intellectual who is decrying his break with the communal past. The community, in African literature, dominates all aspects of African thought. Dances are communal and worship is communal. Property was held communally before the colonial era and there are attempts today to reinstate that practice. This inbuilt bias toward the community means that individualism is always seen as a deviance. Obviously this has had a significant impact on the nature of the institutions and life of society.

Tradition plays a big part in reinforcing the communal ethic. A father tells his son,

> With us, son, the word 'why?' is not a common word. Our tradition never gives an answer because it never asks the question. To it there is only one law in life and that is obedience.[2]

> Tradition is sacred. Custom is above all. To question tradition is sacrilege. If men do not respect tradition how can society stand? How can we be proud of our forefathers and pass on our pride to our children? What would happen if you or I were allowed to change our ancient practices as we like? For us tradition is not a passing thing. It is the earth on which we live and the air which we breathe.[3]

83

Tradition, as you say, is indeed a sword: but it is not a sword that destroys. It is the sword which protects us from the inroads of foreign and dangerous ideas.[4]

Thus the individual is always pitted against the communal tradition. In individual acts such as marriage, he is not free to choose either his partner or the manner of the marriage. To wit,

We have our pride and must do as our fathers did. You see your mother? I did not pick her in the streets. When I wanted a woman I went to my father and told him about my need of her and he went to her father. . . . Marriage is a family affair. You young people of today may think you are clever. But marriage is still a family affair.[5]

This overriding concern with tradition underlines the insecurity and fear of change that lie at its root. Some writers put it very bluntly. 'By sending his son to school and college, he had already opened the way to new and startling ideas.'[6]

Austin J. Shelton, after studying Nzekwu's *Wand of Noble Wood*, Achebe's *No Longer At Ease* and Soyinka's *The Lion and the Jewel*, among other works, has concluded that

The value most clearly approved in these . . . works is traditional communal responsibility revealed partly in the condemnation of self-seeking individualism. Communal responsibility (to the extended family, the clan, the gods) is sanctioned by traditional African societies and furnishes the criteria whereby one can make judgements which will be correct and perform actions which will be justly rewarded. As a value system it is preferred to European individualism. . . . When the African becomes acculturated he either loses a number of his communal values and substitutes for them European individualism, or adds the individualism on to his communalism. But adaptation to the European way can be disappointing, for such change often does not carry with it all the rewards anticipated by the African.[7]

Consider the predicament of the pharmacist Wilson, in Cyprian Ekwensi's *Beautiful Feathers*. As an individual he knows that the money he makes in his pharmacy must be reinvested if it is going to succeed. At the same time, he knows that this is an idle hope, since 'The mild success of his enterprise brought the first flood of Yaniya's relatives with 'give me' hands outstretched. Their in-lawness had become a onesided affair in which they as bride-givers became perpetual recipients of gifts and support from the bride-taker.'[8] It is doubtful whether a social system that makes this kind of demand on the individual is conducive to the accumulation of wealth for development.

Strange acts are sometimes performed in the name of communally based traditions. This is the case with the shooting of Benjamin-Benjamin in *One Man, One Matchet*. We have already pointed out that in Aluko's novel Benjamin-Benjamin is a poorly educated, crooked politician who preys on the illiteracy of the population and swindles a good deal of money. The colonial government, lacking concrete evidence, cannot punish him. However, Chief Olowokere shoots him (and then shoots himself). He explains 'I shot and killed him. . . . An' I do not regret killing Benja-Benja. He was a crook. He ought to have been sent to jail for seven years for the amount of money he stole from the various amounts collected from the people.'[9] Here the Chief is pointing out that the communal code is higher than the concern for any individual or individuals. This is why he kills Benja-Benja and attempts to kill himself. The 'higher' value is the society *in toto*, and not the two individuals. As Mopeli-Paulus has suggested, in another context, no matter how repulsive ritual murder may be, once a chief – in the name of the tribe – appoints someone to do it, the communal obligation is higher than any individual's preference, with the corollary that ultimately it is the chief's responsibility regardless of who actually commits the act.[10]

Those characters who are purely individualistic in African literature, no matter how much good they are doing, always end in tragedy. In depicting the characters in this fashion, African writers are intending to point out that the tradition of the communal ethic is all pervasive, and that those who defy it do so at their own risk. This is the case with Simi 'of the lazy eyes', the prostitute in Soyinka's *The Interpreters*. Here is an independent individualistic character who picks and chooses her lovers. She is urbanised. When after years of playing this game, she picks Egbo as her favourite, he is taken away from her 'by a simple college girl'.[11] Another such character is Ochola in Grace

Ogot's *The Promised Land*. Ochola is an enterprising young man who moves away from a densely populated area to richer agricultural land. Because he has left the communal (tribal) lands, after at first becoming rich he becomes very sick and must leave the riches behind. The disease is regarded by the people as clearly linked to his stay in non-communal land.[12]

In Achebe's *Arrow of God*, Ezeulu, the priest of Ulu (a god) is an individualist. When he refuses the chieftainship offered by the colonial government and when, in spite of the insistence of the clan, he refuses, because he is in prison, to eat the yams which signify the days of the year and thus allow the people to begin harvesting, tragedy follows. As head priest, Ezeulu is bound to follow the tradition in order to prevent disaster in the form of crops rotting in the fields. When he defaults on his responsibility, misfortune strikes. Among other tragedies, his son dies. This is explained by the people as resulting from Ezeulu's rejection of the communal ethic.

> So in the end only Umuaro [the village] and its leaders saw the final outcome. To them the issue was simple. Their god had taken sides with them against his headstrong and ambitious priest and thus upheld the wisdom of their ancestors – that no man, however great, was greater than his people. That no man ever won judgment against his clan.[13]

This seems to be the moral of what happens to Obi Okonkwo, the hero of *Things Fall Apart*. Okonkwo has been entrusted with bringing up Ikemefuna, a hostage from another village. Ultimately, Ikemefuna must be sacrificed. Okonkwo is not supposed to have anything to do with the sacrifice but he accompanies the clan elders when they go to kill Ikemefuna. When the boy is struck and runs toward him, Okonkwo cuts him down because he is 'afraid of being thought weak'.[14] This is the beginning of tragedy for him. Later he accidentally shoots and kills a clansman. He must be exiled and everything he owns is destroyed to appease the tribal gods.[15] This in itself would not be such a disaster if Okonkwo had not all along been basically motivated by the need to achieve wealth and status and thus to rise above his lazy father. This individualistic concern – not to be a nothing like his father – is the explanation given for his tragedies.

The ongoing fear of failing the communal obligation is found even in undertakings like education. A young boy beginning school tells us,

> My father went on to remind me that I have now started to climb a palm tree which was high and difficult to climb; that many were watching my progress, and much ripe fruit was awaiting me on the successful conclusion of my climb. He ended with the warning that if I failed to reach the top, those watching me, both living and the dead, would curse me for failing them. On the other hand, if I reached the top in order simply to gorge myself with fruit, I would surely become sick and fall to the ground and die. But if I returned to my people to share with them the fruits of my labors, then all would sing my praise and honor those who brought me to life.[16]

Note that even if he does well, the honour is not his but goes to his family, clan and tribe.

The primacy of the communal ethic sometimes works well in controlling deviants and forcing them into normalcy. This is, for example, what happens to Danda in Nwanko's novel. Danda is a drunk, therefore he is not able to take care of himself and his family. He stays single until well past the age of marriage, but pressure builds up until he has to marry. Not only does he marry but the pressure of his family ultimately channels his social life into a semblance of stability. He reaches the highest *ozo* level — thus demonstrating that it is possible for a no-good wastrel to rise to a position of prominence within his society through communal coercion.[17]

On the other hand, the communal ethic can definitely hamper the general welfare at times by blocking those who want to work for the general good. It is as if

> Tyranny gathers a whip
> From the timid crowd
> And (with their own dejected fears)
> Molests the weak.[18]

This tyranny is used against Mr Kalaa, in Wilson Mativo's story 'Our True Speaker', who seeks to oust the corrupt Mr Malu from Parliament. The latter — once every election time — exploits the rural population's desire for trifles such as candy and soda at the expense of major principles and improvements such as roads, schools and hospitals.[19] The same tyranny also operates in *When Love Whispers*, to lead an educated woman to marry an illiterate chief because she is going to have a baby out of wedlock.[20] Similarly in *The Looming Shadow*, when a particular person is accused of witchcraft virtually the entire village turns against him.[21]

The literature suggests that the modern African individualist is almost by definition a schizoid person. This word is not used lightly, but arises from the fact that whenever the individual has apparently shaken the operational aspects of the communal ethic, it nevertheless returns to haunt his memory. Lombe, a civil servant whom we encountered earlier, regards the city, which gives him the chance to escape the communal ethic, as also a trap. This it in fact turns out to be since Lombe, in the exercise of his freedom, takes up with a bar girl, impregnates her and finds out ultimately that she is his step-sister. This is a serious taboo and it upsets him seriously. His refuge is the village where the ethic is strongest, and he goes there 'for a long search'.[22]

Three other major characters are portrayed in the same light. One is Obi Okonkwo in *No Longer at Ease*. Obi returns from the United Kingdom confident that he can withstand the pressure of the communal ethic, but ultimately he admits that the clan organisation does have a claim on him. His education was actually through and for them. Therefore he must reward them by living up to their expectations of him – by having a car and a good house, and by placing his relatives in government positions. This ultimately means that he must accept bribes to keep up with 'Mukasas'. After this we are not surprised when he is accused by the clan organisation. However, they are not angry but instead berate him for being cheap – that is, for not having taken bigger bribes more befitting his position.[23]

A perfect example of the schizoid individualist character is Egbo, the fiery aristocrat-nationalist, who works in the Ministry of Foreign Affairs in Soyinka's *The Interpreters*. Egbo originally broke with the communal ethic when he refused to assume title as the next in line in a tribal chieftaincy. Yet he has not been able to sever himself completely from his past.

Perfunctory doles towards the Union of Osa Descendants . . .
messages between the old man and himself . . . all these had
built up ties surreptitiously . . . delegates too, to feel him out,
sent by Egbo Onosa as he knew quite well – destiny they
always said, you were destined. . . . All these and much more
. . . his one overwhelming need to retain that link with some
out-of-the-run existence . . . illicit pleasure at the thought
that a kingdom awaited him whenever he wanted it. . . . And
he only plunged again into the ancient lie of still sediments.
How long will the jealous dead remain among us![24]

Reminded by Bandele that it was he himself who had rejected
the title, Egbo elaborates on the nature of choice open to the
individualist in the African social milieu – a choice which he
feels differs from that afforded in Western social thought. 'Even
that choice is a measure of tyranny. A man's gift of life should
be separate, an unrelated thing. All choice must come from
within him, not from promptings of his past.'[25] This derives
from Egbo's perception of what the past should be. His companion complains, 'You continue to talk of the past as if it has
no place with us.' Egbo replies,

> It should be dead. And I don't just mean bodily extinction.
> No, what I refer to is the existing fossil within society, the
> dead branches on a living tree, the dead runs on the bole.
> When people die, in one sense or the other, it should not
> matter what they were to us. They owe the living a duty to be
> forgotten quickly, usefully. Believe me, the dead should have
> no faces. . . . Is it impossible to seal off the past and let it
> alone? Let it stay in its harmless anachronistic unit so we can
> dip into it at will and leave it without commitment, without
> impositions! A man needs that especially when the present,
> equally futile, distinguishes itself only by a particularly
> objectionable lack of courage. . . . I merely say that the dead
> should be better tucked away. They should not be interferred
> with because then they emerge to thrust terrifying dilemmas
> on the living. They have no business to make impositions on
> us.[26]

But this is not the extent of Egbo's criticism – he is not simply
rejecting the communal ethic which argues that the 'dead, the

living and the yet to be born' have ongoing symbiotic obligations. He draws back from this position, which would be individualistic in the Western sense. He continues,

> If the dead are not strong enough to be everpresent in our
> being, should they not be as they are dead? . . . But what are
> we then . . . to continue making advances to the dead? Why
> should the dead on their part fear to speak to light?[27]

Egbo is pulled by the attraction of the tradition because he feels
it has something to offer – but what? Culture? Opposition to the
barbarity of politicians? He travels toward the Kingdom
intending to make peace but on reaching very close,

> The spectre of generations rose now above him and Egbo
> found he would always shrink, although incessantly drawn
> to the pattern of the dead. And this waiting near the end of
> the journey, hesitating on the brink, whining as he admitted
> it – was it not exhumation of a better past? Belatedly think-
> ing, who am I to meddle? Who? Except – and this counted for
> much – *that he knew and despised the age which sought to mutilate
> his beginnings.*
>
> And there was personal threat to his grandfather but then,
> he did not doubt that the old man understood the political
> risks and would accept reversals. And Egbo wishes, if that
> could be all! If the fight were only political, nothing more.
> But Egbo had felt a virile essence, a redeeming grace in the
> old man and in that existence. And this was being destroyed,
> he knew, and by cozening half-men who came bloated on
> empty wind. There is also pride of race. Egbo said, 'I am after
> all, an Egbo'. . . . [He] had become different at this point,
> waiting to go on shore and grapple with his failure to insu-
> late, different from the distant disillusionment, his fears for
> the dignity of his roots, and the fate of a burnt out fire-eater.
> He acknowledged it finally, this was the place of death. And
> admitted too that he was drawn to it, drawn to it as a dream
> of isolation, smelling its archaic menace, and the violent
> undertows, unable to deny its dark vitality.[28]

As the ambivalence expressed in this quotation suggests, the search for the past often involves a rejection of the values of the present, including individualism, although this may not be what the seeker intends. Egbo later catalogues the advantages of tribal chieftaincy as polygamy, 'hobby' power, and wealth from controlling smuggling routes, but he is not interested in these. In fact, he would be in favour of abolishing the latter if he could secure the help of other young people like himself, but he is convinced that they are not interested since they are

> . . . [t]oo busy, although I've never discovered doing what. And that is what I constantly ask – doing what? Beyond propping up the herald-men of the future, slaves in their hearts and blubber-men in fact, doing what? Don't you ever feel that your whole life might be sheer creek-surface bearing the burden of fools, a mere passage, a mere reflecting medium of occasional sheer mass-controlled ferments beyond you?

Bandele shrugged, 'I don't work in the Civil Service.' 'But you acquiesce in the syste', Egbo says. 'You exist in it, lending pith to hollow reeds.'[29]

Soyinka most clearly points out in this passage that the issue is not just the rejection of the traditional communal ethic, but rather the creation of an atmosphere in society where people acting as individuals can create a new ethic less binding and destructive than the tyranny of tradition. He implies that the failure to achieve this is linked to the rise to power of irrelevant politicians when 'the winds of change blew',[30] and also to the failure of the supremely individualistic intellectuals to acknowledge and come to grips with their duty to the community. The same idea is expressed by Patrick, a character in *Blade Among the Boys*.[31]

In summary, then, the primacy of the traditional communal ethic as opposed to an individualistic ethic continues to dominate the African socio-political milieu. The communal ethic is accepted not only by the traditionalist but is shared by the modern African as well. The latter also accepts the very European principle of efficiency, but it is not at all clear that the two are compatible. Those who follow an independent path are in one way or other eliminated. Yet the intellectuals recognise that in order to be of greatest service to their societies they must break away and establish a milieu where the primacy of the individual is unchallenged and co-exists with a collective social conscience which is not tyrannical.

Part Three: African Identity in the World Context

9 Interpretations of the Past, the Present and the Future

> You are not a country, Africa,
> You are a concept,
> Fashioned in our minds, each to each
> To hide our separate fears,
> To dream our separate dreams.[1]

In dreaming and fearing, each to each, African writers have articulated perceptions of their past, their present and their future in the world context. The past is generally viewed as having two phases – the pre-European past and the colonial past. The writers' perceptions of the present stem basically from the time when African societies began to gain control over their own governments, and not necessarily from the dates of independence. The future, of course, is that which they hope will come. It is important to remember that the concepts past, present and future are not limited here to historical dates. What was perceived as the future in the period of agitation for independence may or may not be included in our schema of the future. It may, alternatively, be included as part of the present, i.e., as part of that which came after the coloniser handed control over society back to the African people.

Most Africans who were educated by Europeans remember the countless times they were told that they had never had any culture of their own and that their societies were barbaric; and they know how, finally, 'black' and 'dark', as applied to the continent and its people, became synonymous with bad. This fact has generated a strong reaction in the literature which seeks to point out that Africa did have a culture and an order in past society. Almost all writers dwell on this theme. We quote

95

only one of them to illustrate the perceptions of the pre-European existence in Africa. Simon Kihohia writes:

There had always been interfamily differences –
Often tacit, sometimes noisy, rarely violent.
Within individual families, cooperation ruled
    supreme;
From each was expected according to his ability,
and this was met by all with alacrity.
To each was issued according to his need,
All this was accepted without a murmur.
The opportunities of life, the fruits of labour,
These were never betrayed to competition.
This had always been the state of affairs,
No less for the peasants than for the elders,
And no more for the men than for the women;
It was likewise between the children and the adults.
That they were not siblings and parents,
Well this was the concern of the Estate.
Individual needs were met in public service.
Let none err – this was virgin communalism,
Handed down by the ancestor to the contemporaries.
It was sacred inheritance for bequest to posterity.[2]

This romantic view is common when Africans write of the pre-European past. It may well be an over-compensation for the denials imposed by the Western world. This opinion is supported by Chinua Achebe, who categorically states that the fundamental theme for the writer 'is that African peoples did not hear of culture for the first time from Europeans',[3] and that the writer's role is 'to help my society regain belief in itself and put away the complexes of the years of denigration and self-abasement'.[4] He concludes by saying that pre-European 'society had its good side – the poetry of life, the simplicity, if you like; the communal way of sharing happiness and sorrow and in work and all that'.[5]

There are admissions in African literature that some aspects of the society, *viewed from today's* perspective, were cruel. However, the emphasis is on what was good about the society. In the sense that the writer seeks to re-create dignity in a peoples' past, *perhaps* the over-romanticisation is understandable. This point should be stressed because critics of the literature point to its over-romanticisation as a major weakness. Perhaps this is its strength; particularly if we accept the principle that the writer seeks to 're-create' a history.[6] It is with this concern in mind for example that Parkes and Armattoe, respectively, exclaim to the European tradition which colonised them,

> Give me black souls,
> Let them be black
> or chocolate brown
> Or make them the
> Colour of dust
> Browner than sand
> But if you can
> Please keep them black
> Black.[7]

and,

> Our God is black!
> Black of eternal blackness,
> With large voluptuous lips,
> Matted hair and brown liquid eyes,
> Figure gainly formed is He,
> For in his image we are made.[8]

The colonising process is seen as one in which honourable but doubting people were hoodwinked by Europeans who were basically tricksters. Rubadiri aptly captures the feeling of hesitancy on the part of the Africans in his poem, *Stanley Meets Mutesa*.

> . . . Such was the welcome
> No singing women to chant a welcome
> Or drums to greet the white ambassador;
> Only a few silent nods from aged faces
> and one rumbling drum roll
> To summon Mutesa's court to parley
> For the country was not sure.
>
> The gate of reeds is flung open
> There is silence
> But only a moments silence –

A silence of assessment
The tall black king steps forward
He towers over the thin bearded white man
Then grabbing his lean white hand
Manages to whisper
'Mtu mweupe karibu'
White man you are welcome

The gate of polished reed closes behind them
And the West is let in.[9]

Rubadiri's description accents what he feels was the almost accidental acceptance of the West by Africa. Looking backward Kwesi Brew is not so sure that it was quite that fatalistic. He suggests in 'The Search' that perhaps the ancestors who let the white man in were simply duped by him.[10]

The fact that the missionary preceded the trader and the governor is expressed in various ways by African writers. Kihohia notes the sequence and argues that the African ancestors were hypnotised:

An officious stranger appeared at our gate,

.   .   .   .

Under apparent hypnotism, we followed him to a shrine
And there under his direction, prostrated ourselves.
Aware of the influence he wielded on us,
He ordered our eyes shut – ostensibly – well, for ritual!
Meanwhile, he dashed off to delimit our estate
Slowly but surely, he strategically lodged himself among us.
Henceforth his brother regularly visited the estate for
    barter –

.   .   .   .

Yielding to vice, the two rascals contrived a privileged position,
And adding an insult to a fault, decided to consolidate it.
Thus they settled and invited a third brother for 'defence'.
Subsequently, our elders and councils were liquidated;
Our commonwealth was pacified and superceded with partnership.
The metamorphosis now complete, the insignia was hoisted
The visitor at the gate was actually a carnivore.[11]

George Awoonor-Williams articulates the same view. He states:

The weaver bird built in our house

. . . .

We did not want to send it away

. . . .

. . . The weaver returned in the guise of the owner
Preaching salvation to us that owned the house
They say it came from the West
And our horizons limit at its nest
But we cannot join the prayers and answers of the communi-
    cants.
We look for new homes everyday
For new altars we strive to rebuild
The old shrines defiled from the weavers' excrement.[12]

The only truly historical novel in African literature deals with the same question of how the coloniser managed to get in. This is Stanlake Samkange's *On Trial For My Country*. Lobengu-la, the last great chief of the Matabele, and Cecil Rhodes are on trial for their respective countries once they cross the river of death. Lobengula is on trial in a court of the previous chiefs and Rhodes in his former parish. What clearly comes out is the trickery of Rhodes against an honourable Chief. The story is told by one of the dead so 'that many people may know'[13] today, and expressions of distrust abound from the Council of Chiefs. For example: 'Don't worry, we know that white men are born liars. Never trust a white man.'[14] 'These white dogs haven't got a single bone of truth in them.'[15] Rhodes admits that he swin-dled Lobengula. 'I frankly admit, therefore, that even as early as when I sent Rudd, Thompson and Maguire to negotiate a mineral concession with Lobengula, I had long before decided to dispossess him of his land and the only question was how.'[16] In this way the African rulers are portrayed as honest, and de-termined to protect their people, but they are deceived, ex-ploited and decimated by the Christian, 'civilised' Rhodes. Thus Samkange can ask, 'Was all this talk about Christianity to make us soft so that they could steal our land? Yes, that is why they made you close your eyes when they prayed – so that when you opened your eyes – the land would be gone!'[17] The colonising process is perceived in African literature as having been pioneered by the missionary and carried on by the trader and the administrator in that order. But since it was the missionary who created havoc with African culture, the writers today totally reject most of the so-called Christian ideals.

Having made the first thrust, the colonisers proceeded to establish their own values and modes of organisation during the colonial era. In doing this Dei-Anang tells us that they 'trampled', 'partitioned' and 'pawned' the continent but they never really mastered it since ultimately it broke away.[18] The colonisers in their activities during the colonial period did not understand African culture. They cumbersomely lived in it, tearing it apart in their crudity. To wit:

> You who are from far-fabled country
> Reached into our virgin jungle
> Passing thro' like therapeutic rays
> Muscles tangled-torn out of roll
> Has the fire stopped riding the wind?
>
> Walk as on your tarmac our occult groves
> With alien care and impunity
> Walk in abandon ahead tourist droves
> Eyes so big like sailors
>   Ranging mirage distance
> To where God in heaven plunges earth
> How can they catch the thousand intricacies
> Tucked away in crannies
> And corners perhaps known only to rats?
> How can they tell the loincloth
> Cast away in heat of desire
> The bits clanging in the wind
>   Now groins want oiling?[19]

Thus, Dei-Anang asserts that Westerners cannot understand the Africans' need to recreate what they see as their own cultural traits. This is the groin needing oil. Europe continues to debase African culture and to offer a few dollars here and there, while the exploitation of the continent's resources for the advantage of Europe continues. To wit:

> Rare works of art discovered in
>   Tin mines! Another at Benin
> Of great historical
> Interest in London, Moscow, New York
> Those unguent gums and oils
> Drawn in barrels off to foreign mills
> The soil quarried out of recognition
> As never would erosion
>   another millenium.[20]

Above all there is protest over the fact that the European powers enslaved black men.

> The blood crying for blood split free
> From keels away on frothing sea
> The dark flesh rudely torn
> And grafted on to red fetid sore
> Breeding a hybrid lot
> To work the land of the sunset.[21]

An even greater bitterness toward the coloniser is expressed in Mabel Segun's 'Second Olympus':

> From the rostrum they declaimed
> On martyrs and men of high ideals
> Whom they sent out
> Benevolent despots to an unwilling race
> Straining at the yoke
> Bull-dozers trampling on virgin ground
> In blatant violation
> They trampled down all that was strange
> And filled the void
> With half-digested alien thoughts,
> They left a trail of red
> Wherever their feet had passed.[22]

Beyond decrying the colonial experience, African writers attempt to discuss how the society reacted to colonialism. It is brought out in the literature that those groups which were traditionally outcasts in African societies were the very ones to identify themselves with the missionaries at the beginning.[23] To the extent that they were ultimately accepted into the colonial establishment as cooks, labourers, clerks, catechists, etc., these

African converts acquired money and their status rose. Thus they developed a sort of middle-class mentality. Another source of division introduced by the missionaries was the distinction between heathens and saved! Ngugi writes,

> Education for Njoroge [son of a laborer], as for many boys of his generation, held the key to the future. As he could not find companionship with Jacobo's children [Jacobo is Christian] (except for Mwihaki), for these belonged to the middle class that was beginning to be conscious of itself as such, he turned to reading.[24]

That way he can escape the fate of his father, working for a white man, or, worse, for an Indian.[25]

Neither European traders nor administrators are dealt with extensively in African literature. The administrators are included in almost every novel as part and parcel of something called government. (See the section on the politicians.)

During the colonial era once the people began to understand that an injustice had been committed against them, it was simply a matter of time before they sought juridical independence. The feeling expressed in African literature is that this juridical independence was a prerequisite to African cultural revival as well as being necessary for the identity of Black peoples all over the world. Agitation for independence was geared to several specific issues. One of the key ones was the desire for land. Ironically the stimulus came from the teachings of the missionaries. Commenting on his character Njoroge, Ngugi writes,

> Equity and justice were there in the world. If you did well and remained faithful to your God, the Kingdom of heaven would be yours. A good man would get a reward from God. . . . The tribal stories told to him by his mother had strengthened this belief in the virtue of toil and perseverance. His belief in a future for his family and the village rested not only on a hope for sound education but also on a belief in a God of love and mercy, who long ago walked on this earth with Gikuyu and Mumbi or Adam and Eve. And with all this there was growing up in his heart a feeling that the Gikuyu people, whose land had been taken by the white men, were

no other than the children of Israel about whom he read in the Bible. So although all men were brothers, the black people had a special mission to the world because they were the chosen people of God. This explained his brother's remark that Jomo was the Black Moses.[26]

It is one of those ironies of history that the ideology of the ruling classes is often adapted by the ruled for ends very different from those it was designed to achieve. Thus the Christian ethic was used by the African for purely political ends.

In trying to shape their peoples identity vis-à-vis the rest of the world, African writers find much to comment on in the two world wars, particularly the Second World War. In Western 'mythology' this war was a war to save democracy from evil. But African writers question that supposition. For example, Abruquah writes:

Look at these British, [we often said in discussion.] They have been calling us apes, too. Now that they want our money for Spitfires, they are saying the Germans are responsible. As for enslavement, what do they think we are now?

Yes, the British are too cunning, [someone would add.] They have been in the Gold Coast more than a hundred years, and what have they taught us? We cannot even make a pin.[27]

Because of the discrimination practised against them even as soldiers, those who fought in the war quickly became the malcontents of the post-war era. They would never again accept the superiority of the white man once they had shot at one. Ngugi writes about one Boro, an ex-soldier:

Boro thought of his father who had fought in the war only to be dispossessed. He too had gone to war against Hitler. He had gone to Egypt, Jerusalem and Burma. He had seen things. He had often escaped death narrowly. But the thing he could never forget was the death of his step-brother, Mwangi. For whom or for what he he died? When the war came to an end, Boro had come home, no longer a boy but a man with experience and ideas, only to find that for him there was to be no employment. There was no land on which he could settle, even if he had been able to do so.[28]

Thus the Boros became the intellectual leaders of the discontent which ultimately led to the mass movements culminating in independence.

The rejection of Europe by the ex-soldiers spread to the intellectuals who rejected 'Europe' *and* the local leaders who had become identified with the coloniser. Although there was often an age difference between the two groups, this was not simply a generational conflict. Osadebay, writing in the early fifties, says in 'Young Africa's Lament':

> I am half starved
> I asked for bread, they gave me stones
> I am thirsty
> I asked for water, they gave me slush . . .
>
> I have no leaders,
> Pretenders would sell me for bread,
> They babble and squabble
> And leave me deaf with empty noise;
> They say I'm young and have no sense,
> to take the way that leads to the goal.
> I waited for them but all in vain.[29]

Osadebay insists that African culture should be preserved for its own good and not because Europeans perhaps find it quaint. It is the following poem, 'Young Africa's Plea', that has led some critics to argue that he rejected his past. In it he writes:

> Don't preserve my customs
> As some fine curios
> To suit some white historian's tastes
> There's nothing artificial
> That beats the natural way
> In culture and ideals of life.
> Let me play with white man's ways
> Let me work with the black man's brains
> Let my affairs themselves sort out.
> Then in sweet rebirth
> I'll rise a better man
> Not ashamed to face the world.
> In secret fear my strength
> They know I am no less a man.

Let them bury their prejudice
Let them show their noble sides
Let me have untramelled growth
My friends will never know regret
And I, I never once forget.[30]

These lines were addressed to the one,

Who chained my feet, asleep,
Plucked my wings so bare
(Designing to foil)
And says my past is blank . . .
That I have no ambition
To fly.[31]

At the same time, Osadebay admits that the traditions of Africa, just like the role of Europe, are under fire by the new generation seeking recognition in the world as a people. As spokesman for the new Africa, he says,

. . . I am a critic
And never take for granted,
Assumptions of my fathers' days
Are stumbling blocks across my ways;
To clear them is my duty call,
To walk erect and never crawl.

My simple fathers
In childlike faith believed all things;
It costs them much
And I their offspring lost a lot;
They questioned not the lies of magic,
And fetish seemed to have logic
They were deceived by first appearance
And now I need deliverance.[32]

The issue of identity in the early 1950s was not as yet independence. It was, instead, the desire for dignity and for observance of the 'rights of man' in the existing state of affairs. For example:

I do not crave for riches
Nor wordly pomp and power,
I ask for God's free air

And shelter from the elements;
Give me these rights of man,
The right to think my thoughts,
The right to say my views
The right to stand erect
And call my soul my own,
Then let a fitting throne
My humble heart provide
Where kindness may abide.[33]

One poem in which all of these themes merge is Francis Ernest Kobina Parkes' 'Two Deaths, One Grave'. He writes:

The root of this world's strife
Is greed
Man's greed
It has nothing to do with colour
Black or white or yellow or green
Man dies because man kills

.　　.　　.　　.　　.　　.

(Black) man dies because
(White) man kills

Kills body and soul
Then finds justification
In euphemisms

.　　.　　.　　.　　.　　.　　.

Hiroshima and Nagasaki smiled
As they send bullets through his back . . .

What had Communism to do with death,
The many weak queried.

Everything
The strong replied
Everything
Hungary . . .
Siberia . . .
Nuclear Tests . . .

And he took the cue and continued:

Suez . . .
1914 . . .
1939 . . .
Berlin today and yesterday
Where the few strong took hold
Of the many weak of Africa
and partitioned them up like venison . . .[34]

The literature provides many examples of the Africans' opinion of the coloniser, and suggests why that opinion developed European characters in these works who are generally depicted as anti-African, which is why they are resented. The point need not be laboured since the horse is already dead. Mr Green, Obi Okonkwo's boss in *No Longer At Ease*, states:

> The African is corrupt through and through. . . . They are all corrupt, [repeated Mr Green]. I for one would hate to live in South Africa. But equality won't alter facts. . . . The fact that over countless centuries the African has been the victim of the worst climate in the world and of every imaginable disease. Hardly his fault. But he has been sapped mentally and physically. We have brought him Western education. But what use is it to him.[35]

Mrs Brown, married to an expatriate officer who brings his African assistant to tea just prior to independence, expresses her feelings lucidly.

> Do you know we had one of those gangs of hooligans coming here to shout again. . . . Yes, awful slogans – *Kwacas* and freedom. Can't the police do something about it? Why can't they lock up that Native leader of theirs? I really cannot understand what all this is about. It was alright in India – they had a lot of fairly educated men in their country even though they had to have European supervision – but who can run a government here? I am sure you are not one of them, Mr Loni? I mean your people still have got a long way to go.[36]

Although her husband is 'enlightened', Mrs Brown clearly is not. It is this type of talk to which the literature mainly reacts. Another example of the European expatriate is found in Jame Ngugi's *Grain of Wheat*, where the foreigner is described as making the categorical statement that: 'Africa cannot, cannot do without Europe.'[37]

Patronising Europeans are told in the literature in one way or another that what they value in terms of the 'European' contribution to Africa may really be irrelevant. Dei-Anang, writing in 1946, summed it up best in 'Africa Speaks':

> The dazzling glare of iron and steel
> Sometimes obscures non-metal worth;
> So when I disdained my pristine
> Bows and arrows
> And cared not much for iron and steel
> They called me 'Dark' in all the world
>
> But dearer far than cold steel and iron
> Is the tranquil art
> Of thinking together
> And living together.[38]

This is a neat inversion of the argument that modernisation leads to greater humanity.

Whereas the writers' arguments about the African past centre on the process of colonisation and the role oi the African and the European then and in the subsequent colonial period, their criticisms and ideas about the present are not mainly directed against Europe. They are directed rather toward European Africa – that is to say Africa corrupted by the colonial legacy. Wilson of *Beautiful Feathers* states:

> In the old days the African had a bond with an Ultimate Being. Then came 'civilization,' that took away the older religion and substituted something new and unstable. Now that which the white man had substituted has gone. There was nothing. At moments like this the New Black Man – he was one of them – was alone. Alone![39]

This is the loneliness of the cultural dilemma posed by the fact that although Europe is rejected in the colonial revolution, the African cannot go back to traditional societal systems because, above all, the continent must be developed [which to this writer anyway seems to be largely a European value!]. Africans are lonely because as Lenrie Peters says in 'In The Beginning',

> We heard the politicians
> Saviours of a nation
> Of the race
> We saw
> bitterness of our hearts
> in their eyes
> their days of sorrow
> years of prison
>
> .   .   .   .   .   .
>
> We heard
> about socialism
> the equal sharing of goods
> freedom, the new Africa
> the African personality
>
> .   .   .   .   .
>
> meanwhile
> the Politicians came and went
> Meteors about the sky
>
> .   .   .   .   .   .
>
> the common income fell
> the death rate stayed alive
>
> .   .   .   .   .
>
> they promised once
> led us to believe
> it was our only hope
> We starved as slaves, colonials
> then home-made slaves again.[40]

During the colonial interlude, it was easy and fashionable to criticise Europe wholesale, but in the present there is some doubt as to whether it may not in fact be necessary for *The Blind Steersmen* to copy European democracy. Parkes writes,

> Sanity lies in submitting to the bittersweet dream created in factories of democracy by tired, drained-dry brains, doped to senselessness by fact effacing ether.[41]

Yet there is always hope that the fabled masses will come to the rescue, since,

> Everytime the conceited few
> Decide they know best
> And ought to set the pace

> The lazy crowd makes haste
> To put them in their place.[42]

The quest for identity during the present post-independence period is more diversified than in previous periods and embodies more than just race and culture. Consider the following statement by an up and coming intellectual addressing a Briton:

> I'm a typical Congolese gentlemen. I call myself a dedicated vindicator of African personality and I've got my Anglo-Saxon political and academic titles to prove it . . .

> Politically I bark hardest; economically I am bitten hardest. My political constitution is written but my physical constitution is rotten. . . . I love my flag devotedly and you obey yours implicitly. When the whistle blows once, we kiss our flags. When it blows twice we stop kissing it. When it blows thrice we start urinating. When it blows four times – we stop urinating. And when it blows five times we start cutting each others' throat for reasons you and I haven't the faintest idea of . . . Why should we give our love to each other when we have flags to lavish it upon? – Then, we both form a Commonwealth in which wealth is not common.[43]

This deep disillusionment with the inability of society to provide direction for its people is very common in the writers' perceptions of the present. John Ekwere probably is the most blunt. He states openly that the failure of African societies today to affirm their own cultures is their own individual failure and cannot be blamed on Europe. Thus,

> Now no more the palefaced strangers
> With unhallowed feet
> The heritage of our fathers profane;
> Now no missioned benevolent despots
> Bull-doze an unwilling race;
> No more now the foreign hawks
> On alien chickens prey –
> But we on us.[44]

The responsibility for the resolution of the contradictions of the present stalemate – in which African societies are suffering from the mismanagement and corruption imposed by the politicians with the acquiescence of the masses, the bureaucracy and the intellectuals – is placed by Albert Kayper Mensah partly on the present generation, and partly on a future generation unschooled in the ambivalences of the present, which will not be blown helplessly about by the winds of change like their predecessors. We quote:

> This is not a time for jesting
> But for living as they did,
> When our forebears had to save
> The very ethos of the race.
> These are the days when men must speak.
> Shout the meaning of their souls
>
> .   .   .   .
>
> What you suffer in your day
> Is the price you have to pay
> As you try to come to rest
> From the swaying force of change.
> You must learn what life can teach you.
> And remember this my son . . .[45]

Finally, with respect to the future, African writing has stressed the need for political, economic and social freedom in the world context, these to be brought about with the aid of the West.

The hope of development is therefore one of the key elements in the writers' perceptions of the future. This should be understood in two contexts. One is the historical need to refute the assertion that the African is childlike, if not a child in fact, and the other is the fact that one of the major arguments for independence has been that Africa's resources can at last be used for African development. To even entertain the notion, therefore, that development might not occur is to admit that the argument for independence was not true. K. A. B. Jones–Quartey in 'Stranger, Why Do You Wonder So' enunciates this argument.

> Take heart, O Stranger to our land,
> Tomorrow, we shall have the forest cleared,
> The vulture will espy no dung,
> The Child and Mother will be clothed

The snake will turn its poison on itself,
The small tree-bear look down
From museum walls, without a cry.

Give us but the tomorrow,
Make way for Africa in the march
To heaven or to hell.

And would that make you wonder less,
O Stranger to our land?[46]

In spite of the need for development, however, some writers question whether modern technology and what seem to be its associated evils are worth while. J. P. Clark writes:

Pass on then, O pass on, missile hurled
In your headlong flight to fool the world;
Being self-tuned, you never heard
Above our wild herd
And market murmur of assembled waves
A song strange fallen out of night-caves
Like star all of sudden from sky.

I, reared here on cow dung floor
From antedeluvian shore
Heard all, and what good it did
          Magnificent obsession
Now magic chords are broken!

Pass on in mad headlong flight
O pass on, your ears right
Full of throttle sound
So winding up your kaleidoscope
Leave behind unhaunted sleep
An innocent sleep of the ages.[47]

This rejection of the technology and values of the West is clearer in 'Whither Bound Africa', written in 1946, in which Dei-Anang asks:

Forward! To what?
The slums, where man is dumped upon man;
Where penury
And misery

Have made their hapless homes,
And all is dark and drear?
Forward! To what?
The factory
To grind hard hours
In an inhuman mill,
In one long ceaseless spell?

Forward! To what?
To the reeking round
Of medieval crimes,
Where the greedy hawks
O *Aryan stock*
Prey with bombs and guns
On men of *lesser breed*?
Forward to CIVILIZATION

Forward, to dusty tools
And sordid gains,
Proved harbingers
Of mortal strife?

Or forward to crafty laws
Of Adam Smith
That turn the markets upside down
And steel men's hearts
To hoard or burn
The food supplies of half the world
E'en when the other half must starve?[48]

Criticism of what the writers see as an unjustifiable preoccupation on the part of African countries with the technology of the West, when there are blacks oppressed on this earth, is the only major subsidiary theme concerning the future. Africa is seen as the drum major in the crusade to humanise life on earth.

Hear oh ye nations, the drum of Africa calls
And will you not march forth to join this
        great crusade?

.   .   .   .

Will your ingenious mind
Deep sunk in nature's conquest

How to subdue the atom
Colonize the moon
Not rise to hear the call of one distressed?

. . . .

Hail Strijdom,

. . . .

The voice of the oppressed is no more heard

. . . .

Gone is the talking drum
The voice is shrunk
Live glorious spectre, live on, live on . . .
Pale Hiroshima, lay not down your head![49]

This position is paradoxical, because we have seen that Africa has not established itself internally, and yet it calls down upon itself the duty to provide moral leadership for the world. The technology of the West is rejected as a worthwhile value but it is not clear that there is an alternative. It is not enough to implore the African to be more human in the future without showing how.

One is therefore forced to conclude that the search in African writing in the past, the present and the future does not offer concrete proposals concerning socio-political systems. It is basically a reacting process in which the decapitation of traditional culture by the Europeans is projected as evil. It is not clearly portrayed how the European managed to get in. Some writers say the ancestor was drugged, others hypnotised, others tricked, and others that he admitted the European willingly and in good faith without knowing the consequences. The colonial interlude is seen as one in which the European, particularly the missionary, broke down the culture indiscriminately and also oppressed the colonised economically and politically. The two world wars and especially the Second World War shook the African into questioning more and more the role that had been delegated to him. The barbarism of the Second World War also hastened the rejection of Western values and the technology which ultimately led to Hiroshima.

The present period is dominated by the winds of change, with almost all the writers expressing an abhorrence for the politicians and their rule. African literature stresses the need for people to participate in the political system in order to check the politicians who are perverting the culture and with it any opportunity for improving the commonwealth. The future, in African writing, is a mythical conception of Africa leading the rest of the world in its human institutions and in development. But the most persistent theme, is the cry for recognition of the African person and culture by the rest of the human race. The cry is for an African 'Consummation', that is to say, a shedding of cultural inferiority coupled with recognition by the rest of the world as cultural equals:

> When we make our grand finale
> Will there be souls this side of eternity
> Who will wish us fulfillment
> And watch the holy prostration
> And bend and anoint the sinning heads?
> Cannot we join the ceremony of our death
> And partake of the rituals?
> Cannot we carry the remainder of our circumcision
> Away with us beyond?
> The wind blows on the graves
> Sweeping the sparky debris away
> Cannot we find where they buried our birth chord?[50]

10 Pan-Africanism

> Here we stand
> infants overblown
> poised between two civilizations
> finding the balancing irksome,
> itching for something to happen,
> to tip us one way or the other,
> groping in the dark for a helping hand
> and finding none . . .[1]

Pan-Africanism as a social and political idea can be understood on many levels. Probably the most important one is the aspect of cultural unity – the assumption that all African cultures are basically similar. This idea is so common in the literature that it does not need proof. All of the writers use the term 'African' in the place of national or tribal designations each time they wish to juxtapose the countries on that continent with countries in other parts of the world. The fact that they do not choose to state the specific country or the particular people can only be interpreted as their understanding that in their use of terminology they must imply the values which argue for the cultural unity of Africa as a whole.

Pan-Africanism on another level can be understood as a guide to the ordering of personal behaviour vis-à-vis the world outside the continent. This of course means partiality to Africa rather than, for example, America or Asia. Consider the statement by a schoolboy, Kofi, in Akosua Abbs' *Ashanti Boy*:

I want to do well in exams, because I want to help everybody here. I must be a doctor, an engineer, or a lawyer to help. Now all the doctors, engineers and lawyers are Europeans, or nearly all of them, and they can't know us and our troubles as well as we know ourselves. There are not enough of them

117

anyway, and they always go home in the end. They do not stay here . . . We will get self-government one day. We will govern ourselves. Then we must have as good a government as you [Europeans] and you must say, 'Those are good men, as good as us, so of course, their country will be as good as ours and they will be our equals!'[2]

One should note that the motivation is for the African to prove himself to the European, and hence any failure by some Africans is perceived as a failure of the race. It is still a fact, as pointed out earlier, that most African thought is basically of a 'reacting' nature.

Still a third level of perception of Pan-Africanism is the fact that African writers see the problems in every country as similar. This idea is usually coupled with the belief that the 'European' created many states out of what was already an existing unity. Of course, the writers admit that there may be corruption of one sort or another in all African governments, 'things fall apart'[3] in all the countries, and politics and politicians dominate in all. Thus, when Okolo in Gabriel Okara's *The Voice* sets out in quest of truth and justice, he does not confine his travels to one country.[4]

Certain aspects of the traditional societies which hamper the growth of cultural and personal unity across tribal and national lines are viciously attacked by the writers. In so doing they implicitly support the idea of Pan-Africanism. For example, Grace Ogot in *The Promised Land*, makes it clear that she deplores the superstition which prevents Ochola's family from keeping the wealth they have acquired in a land which does not belong to the tribe and which is furthermore in a different 'nation'.[5] Cyprian Ekwensi approves of Jagua Nana's travels and trade in different countries, since in that way she brings fashion and culture to housewives who would not otherwise have it. At the same time he approves of Freddie marrying a non-national because in the last analysis all Africans are one.[6]

The concept of Pan-Africanism has always been put forward as a substitute for tribalism, which is by definition (in the African context) evil. There is, in fact, a contradiction between Pan-Africanism and nation building which is antithetical to tribalism, but that is the subject of another study. What is of concern here is the fact that African writers applaud those who reject the tribal restrictions which pervade such crucial institutions as marriage. Here the writers wish to suggest that the breaking of tribal limitations in social relationships is a prerequisite to the building of a Pan-African society. Thus in the play *Dear Parent and Ogre* the marriage of Siata and Sekou across tribal lines is justified in the final analysis by the fact that the younger generation seeks a better understanding among peoples so as to be able to stand firm before the outside world.[7]

Beyond perceptions such as these on the part of African writers, there is the spectre of South Africa, the symbol of White racism, as a catalyst to ideas on Pan-Africanism. It seems to be the consensus among the writers that until South African blacks gain socio-political rights, African independence in the rest of the continent will remain juridical only and not substantive in terms of race. That is to say, implicit in the existence of racist South Africa is the idea that Africans are not fit to rule themselves. This is a denial of independence for all Africa, given the historical prejudices of the White world. Thus part of the *raison d'être* of Pan-Africanism is to work for the termination of the South African regime and of the elements supporting it.

William Conton writes about Kisimi Kamara who sets out to help in this Pan-Africanist quest. It should be noted that Kisimi Kamara is a prime minister of a country called Songhai. It is not an accident that his country is named Songhai. The author had in mind the ideological influence of the name on Africans who look backward to history and to the once very powerful and learned kingdom of Songhai for inspiration. In the novel, while Kamara is studying in England he meets and falls in love with a South African white girl, Greta Halas.[8] The girl's brother, Jan Halas, and her fiancé, Friedrick Hertog, disapprove of the relationship so much that the latter kills her – running both of them down with his car.[9]

Later, when Kisimi Kamara becomes prime minister he remembers his pre-England vow to work for: '. . . the ideal of helping to create in our time a nation which would achieve both strength and freedom through unity, and the subordination to the ideal of all tribal loyalties.'[10] This goal, coupled with the need to avenge the death of Greta and the appeal by South African Blacks for a loan[11] from a Pan-African Heads of

State Conference in which he has been involved, ultimately lead Kamara to give up the Prime Ministership to travel in South Africa in order to hasten change – change toward a 'United States of Africa'.[12] Learning the language[13] and the geography of South Africa,[14] he leaves his own country illicitly, smuggling a diamond for future use, and gets into South Africa legally as a sightseer.[15] But his purpose is defeated. His plan had been to organise a boycott, but the Blacks in South Africa refuse to have anything to do with him.

Conton could not have chosen a more effective way of pointing out the difficulties involved in organising Pan-Africanism as a political force.

> This, said the Congress leaders, was their quarrel, no one else's. They were asking us for a loan, not a gift. They did not deny their relative inexperience in launching widespread popular campaigns of this type. But in insisting that they should manage the whole business themselves they were seeking above all to confine the tensions within the Union, and not involve the rest of Africa more than necessary at this stage. The Union Government could do nothing about a private loan to the Congress from a group of other political parties. But if it were able to lay hands on a foreigner coming to South Africa on such a mission as I proposed, its vindictiveness would know no bounds.[16]

Kamara therefore goes to find Friedrik Hertog, most likely to kill him, but the book ends in the following manner on the eve of the boycott:

> When I caught up with him he was weaving across the street in wide serpentine movements. I followed him at a distance of a few paces, relishing the mere knowledge that he was at last completely in my power. Then suddenly he stumbled over a curb and fell heavily. He lay very still as I stood over him, and as the first drums began to send their throbbing message across the night it was pity I found in my heart for him, not hate. I stooped quickly, lifted him gently, and bore him through the easing rain to the safety of his home.[17]

Thus we do not know what role Kamara eventually plays in the revolution but we do know that he was at least willing to give up a prime ministership for a Pan-African idea – granted that he did have a personal motive as well.

Other writers seem to imply that although political leaders may be committed to Pan-Africanism, petty and personal concerns often get in the way. Consider for example the case of Wilson Iyari. He is a pharmacist and leader of the Nigerian Movement for African and Malagasy Solidarity. He tells us the motivation for his Pan-Africanism:

> When African Solidarity is eventually achieved there will be hundreds of new pharmacies everywhere on the continent. There will be research schemes into African herbs, roots, barks – the results will be *Africa's own contribution to medical science. At the moment pharmacy is waiting for Africa's contribution*.[18]

But Iyari never sees his expectations materialise for several reasons. His wife runs away with his children, one of whom dies. Secondly, the organisation of which he is the head calls for a demonstration against the government for not doing enough to further the course of solidarity, and there is a full-scale riot! Worse yet, Iyari is appointed by the Prime Minister to go to an international conference to represent his country and to work for ideas to bring about 'solidarity'. All is well until the delegates go hunting.

> Wilson led the Nigerian team and from other parts of Africa very important people formed the team. Americans, Russians, British and French observers brought up the rear – as gunbearers. Wilson saw now that things were working in reverse. The black man could hold his head high; one of the many joys of independence, reversing the course of history.
>
> The white men did not complain, but were silent, and no one suspected anything. Occasionally they met and whispered among themselves or laughed. Wilson called aside a delegate and tried to tell him: 'Look, the world is watching and listening. We must behave our best!' '*Non compres pas.*'
>
> The delegate shrugged his shoulders and walked off into the woods, and at that moment a huge beast shaped like a rhino, but infinitely more elegant, came charging down towards them. Wilson fired, but he also heard the sound of other shots, three or four – before the beast stumbled, leaving

a trail of blood-shattered shrubs and indistinct footprints which they followed till they came to the riverside.

Wilson was among the first to reach the dead beast. It was a very rare specimen and no one could name it, but everyone believed it was highly prized. Some of the hunters wanted the horns, some wanted the whole beast preserved in a museum, and immediately an argument arose and voices became loud. Nobody knew who squeezed the trigger. There was a sharp crack of a shot and everyone ran for cover. Confusion spread.

Wilson saw the white men carrying off the beast and running down the slope. He aimed at the retreating white men, but a shot struck him in the ribs and he fell. He lay there in a shot-riddled mist, choking for breath, while his body floated in endless circles, weightless.[19]

Later he goes to report to the Prime Minister.

'I have come to report to you as ordered, sir. Hem! . . . The conference went quite well, sir. We were in agreement over the main points on the agenda. It was when we came to sport, when we wanted to relax . . .'

Briefly he recounted the hunting episode, culminating in shooting and looting by white men.[20]

The ideas relating to Pan-Africanism in this excerpt need no interpretation. They are self-explanatory.

In summary, then, Pan-African ideas are implied when the writers accent the African rather than the national or the tribal. The writers stress the need for cultural unity to provide a counter-weight to the outside world on one level and to check the disintegrating forces of tribalism on another. Dominating all of these is the identity crisis associated with the continued existence of the South African government which implies inferiority of black peoples everywhere. Finally, there is the idea that 'outsiders', be they Americans, Britons, Frenchmen, Russians or members of any other national group, take advantage of the lack of Pan-African solidarity for their own gains. Most writers suggest that there is collusion in these actions. The Pan-African ideal is held up as a future value to be struggled for, even though it may entail individual or national sacrifice at times. It is only after its achievement that 'We Calibans will inherit the earth.'[21]

11 Social Change

Social change is a synergistic process for which there is no adequate theory. However, looking backward historically, one can always attempt to point out what probably happened and what were the causes or effects. African writers have looked backward and tried to understand when and how 'the rain began to beat'[1] them – that is to say how and by whom traditional society was brought to an end, who or what accelerated the change, and in the colonial period, what groups were involved in bringing about the biggest change – independence. Finally, the writers have looked at the past and the present with an eye to what should be in the future.

This chapter will not only attempt to illustrate the above suggestions but it will also present a summary of previous chapters, examining in particular the relationship of the various groups and ideas to the process of change which has been going on in Africa for the past hundred or so years. This process has been one of changing the society from a particular set of socio-politico-economic relationships and beliefs into another set. The process is still going on. The material presented in this chapter will be loosely organised historically, covering the continent's evolution from a pre-colonial to a colonial status, and from a colonial to an independent status. Finally, a discussion of the requisites of change for the future will be included. The historical organisation is necessarily loose because there are no dates involved. Social change to the extent that it is synergistic by definition can only be viewed as a spiral dialectic whose cut-off points are not clear. Social change is not unilinear or caused only by one agent. It also comes at different rates for different individuals and institutions. Sociologically then the limits of change are always clear *a posteriori* – a fact which should be imparted more thoroughly to theoreticians of development.

In the process of transition the first perceived harbingers of change were the missionaries. The missionaries were not accepted when they came. We are told that they were not even allowed to build their missions among the people, but were relegated instead to those places which the population had no use for because they were thought to be the domain of spirits, the 'Evil Forest'.[2] Of more concern to us, however, are the types of Africans who went to the churches and copied the strange ways. The white man initially converted a few, but 'None of his converts was a man whose word was heeded in the assembly of people. None of them was a man of title. They were mostly the kind of people that were called *efulefu*, worthless empty men.'[3] Thus these early converts could not speak for society since they were of the lowest class. Below them were only the real outcasts. The latter for a period were not recognised by the new converts but as Achebe points out later, 'The two outcasts shaved off their hair, and soon they were the strongest adherents of the new faith. And what was more, nearly all the *osu* [outcasts] in Mbanta followed their example.'[4]

Thus the honour of social leadership is vindicated by the African writers. They knew what to protect in their societies, at least in the initial contact. This had damaging consequences, though. Another writer, emphasising the 'outcast' nature of the first converts, points out one of the results.

> When the Christian missionaries first came our parents thought them queer and wouldn't send us to school. Outcasts and poverty-stricken people went to them. Our parents sent their slaves. The result was that they became the first people to learn how to read and write, wear good dresses and make plenty of money; but they also misrepresented our traditions to them.[5]

As we see, one of the consequences was that the missionaries learned a mixed-up version of the nature and institutions of Africa. Thus when they wrote about them for the West they misrepresented them partly because of the unreliability of their sources if not entirely because of their own prejudices.

Secondly, the conversion of the lowest ranking members of the society is seen by the writers as having produced an inversion of status roles. Those who were outcastes before could now read. They had money and above all they lived in houses similar to those of the Europeans. To the extent that the white man became identified with power and status, and the converts aped him, they also became the ones with status and power within their communities. Traditional leaders were soon sending their sons to acquire the attributes of the white man. This is the decision of Ezeulu in Achebe's *Arrow of God*:

> The place where the Christians built their place of worship was not far from Ezeulu's compound . . . He was not sure what to make of it. At first he thought that since the white man had come with great power and conquest it was necessary that some people should learn the ways of his own deity. . . . But now Ezeulu was becoming afraid that the new religion was like a leper. Allow him a handshake and he wants an embrace. Ezeulu had spoken strongly to his son who was becoming more strange everyday. [He is the effeminate son who has joined the Christians above his father's objections.] Perhaps the time had come to bring him out again. But what would happen if, as many of the oracles prophesied, the white man had come to take over the land and rule? In such a case it would be wise to have a man of your family in his band.[6]

Another example is Waiyaki, son of Chege and descendant of a famous seer, Mugo, who had been ignored by the people when he prophesied that the white man would remove them from their lands. Chege tells his son,

> Arise. Heed the prophecy. Go to the Mission place. Learn all the wisdom and all the secrets of the white man. But do not learn his vices. Be true to your people and the ancient rites. . . . A man must arise and save the people in their hour of need. He shall show them the way: he shall lead them.[7]

Thus the traditional leaders and others with influence in the society joined the missionaries after their power and status positions began to be threatened by those who previously had not mattered.

The traditional elites did not welcome either Christianity or the new ways associated with it – education, especially.

Hence, those who were sent to the mission schools were often the misfits, as William Conton points out:

> My family sent me to school – the only child in our family thus favoured. Perhaps the reason was merely that when the children squatted on the bare earth in front of the house, taking turns in inventing stories, mine always seemed to be the lengthiest and most involved as well as most popular. But my elder brother had learned to give my mother's customers their correct change at an earlier age than I, and one of my younger brothers could beat the drum better than I could. I see now that. . . .[8]

Kobina Afram in *The Catechist*, was sent to school because of the accident of being born with soft hair like a white man – a nutritional deficiency.[9] In *The Only Son* it is the son of a widow who goes to the Mission school, not the sons of those who are established.[10] Thus, Western education, which was tied to Christianity and hence to the missions for most of the colonial period, was a preserve for the underprivileged. One can speculate that this perhaps affords a partial explanation of the fact that the missionary educated, who were outside the traditional elites, were later to become prominent in the nationalist movements.

There is little African writing on social relationships in the colonial interlude other than during the genesis of the nationalist movement, which, in terms of years, is fairly recent. Perhaps in the future the writers will deal more extensively with this period – from the original collision of cultures to the start of the push toward independence.

A few books, such as *The Catechist* by Joseph W. Abruquah, stress the tribulations and trials of a convert who was used by the colonial missionaries as 'God's cannon fodder'. His is a series of hardships – being underpaid, believing in traditional religion as well as in Christianity, and despised by both the missionaries and those he sought to convert.[11] But much new writing remains to be done on this period indicating specifically when, why and how education became an article of faith with the masses.

In the colonial period those who allied themselves with the administration automatically became agents of social change. This is not because they had an ideology of change or because their perceptions were exceptionally good. Most of the time they were simply unwitting accomplices. Consider the Obi (chief) in Nzekwu's *Highlife for Lizards*. He is not a traditional ruler in the strict sense but is rather a creation of Lugard's 'dual mandate', in which the offices of chiefs were established in order to enforce indirect rule. When the market women threaten to strike – they are being forced by the administration to pay for water – it is the Obi who comes to the rescue of the administration and in this way acts as an 'enforcer' of change. The African clerk for the District Officer knows that for reasons of his own the Obi will enforce the change. He says to the District Officer, 'I'm sure the Obi has a very high regard for you and he is looking for an opportunity to demonstrate it.'[12] The Obi calls the women to a meeting and speaks:

> . . . We must not lose sight of the fact that our town needs development. Those of us who have travelled to places like Lagos and Calabar will assure you that white men meant well when they brought us pumps. If we understand it that way it behoves us to show appreciation to these people who left their country and families and seven forests and seven deserts to bring us their own civilization and initiate us into their own wizardry.
>
> You will appreciate that the power house costs money, the pipes cost money and pumps cost money. Those people who work at the power house and those who repair damages to the equipment earn salaries. The drug with which the water is purified does not fall from the skies and it is not picked up in the streets either. Now how do you want to enjoy good, pure water, and refuse to contribute toward it provision?[13]

The Obi is successful in convincing the women to change their traditions for the better of the community. Although, given the logic of the nationalist movement, he is reactionary, yet he brings about critical change in the area of the health and welfare of his people.

The same is true of Jacobo, a preacher and a pyrethrum farmer in Ngugi's *Weep Not Child*. Both occupations catapult him into an emergent middle class. It is highly unlikely that Jacobo would have started farming a cash crop in the first place had he not been a Christian and therefore educated and open to change. Moreover, however repulsive one may find Jacobo's middle class mentality, he is an innovator.[14] Others who were forced by economic circumstances to become innovators are depicted in African literary works. This includes especially those who had to move from their traditional society to go and work in other countries in mining or industry.

Such was the case of one Monare, who had to leave Lesotho and travel all over South and southeastern Africa in Mopeli-Paulus' *Blanket Boy*. Monare is representative of all Africans who went to the mines, were taught some industrial skills, and if they chose, for the rest of their lives, functioned in the industrial sector. They could go back to the reserves, but even when they went back they took with them to the rural and traditional sectors habits learned in the city, whether good ones or bad. They learned new values. Monare, for example, learns about the religious differences between Pathans and the Moslems, the Roman Catholics and the Hindus. All these and many more values made up the configuration acquired by the migrants during the colonial period and were woven by them into the traditional rural societies.[15]

African writers seem to agree that some of the ways of the city are bad, but other urban values such as monogamy and the acquisitive instinct they treat quite positively, possibly in the hope that they will spread more to the rural areas.

Another carrier of change, historically, has been the soldier. Napoleon's *canaille* soldiers made havoc with the accepted mores of Europe during his time. African soldiers from both wars, and from the earlier period of the conquest of Africa, have perhaps contributed more to social change than any other group. Those soldiers who were used during the colonising years, the literature tells us, were basically from the 'slave' tribes, who also ultimately formed the first ranks of African civil servants. The soldiers who fought in the First World War came back and ventured into trade, farming and other areas.[16] They had seen the 'world' and the ideas they picked up stayed with them. However, it was not until the Second World War that large numbers of African soldiers saw service outside the continent. When they came back they resented the favouritism shown the white soldiers. But, above all, they resented their economic plight, which was largely the result of the post-war recession. Consider the case of Boro, in Ngugi's *Weep Not Child*:

> Boro thought of his father who had fought in the war only to be dispossessed. He too had gone to war, against Hitler. He had gone to Egypt, Jerusalem and Burma. He had seen things. He had often escaped death narrowly. But the thing he could not forget was the death of his stepbrother, Mwangi. For whom or what had *he* died?[17]

People like Boro formed that critical, discontented element which is necessary before drastic social change can take place. They were the backbone of the cadres of the political parties which emerged in the fifties. Where there were riots and strikes they formed Lenin's Vanguard. Thus we are not surprised when we find that General R. (short for Russian) in James Ngugi's *A Grain of Wheat* is an ex-soldier who had been a commando in Burma.[18] The change these ex-soldiers achieved was the attainment of dignity for themselves. Once they had taken part in the White man's war they could never again crawl. They and the plight of their families were used by the up and coming politicians in the indoctrination of the masses as examples of exploitation. How could warriors be treated with such neglect, the people later asked. The soldiers had been granted equality – the right to die in battle – and from then on they would not accept retrogression. They became propagandists for independence. Consider Njoka Maki. We are told by Aubrey Kachigwe that the then night watchman for *Kawacha News* started the nationalist movement in his country:

> Njoka Maki started all this. . . . He travelled widely in his early days, first as a soldier and later on his own. He's always elusive. They can't get him for what they want him. . . . Njoka Maki has been in and out of jail almost at his will. He has done things and your father is his disciple. Njoka Maki predicted about what is now taking place many years ago and we thought he was mad. . . . Perhaps that is why he has kept on his road for so long. It's no easy task, my son, to tread on their road. No easy task. That is why your father, her husband, and all these good men are locked in there.[19]

They are in prison because they are nationalists. Njoka Maki has been going into prison so as to indoctrinate and recruit the inmates into the nationalist movement![20]

Other groups played similar critical roles in the process of social change during the latter part of the colonial period. One of these was the town marginal group. In this category were the prostitutes and the market women. We have already described the involvement of Sleepy Aunt, who finances a nationalist movement in *No Easy Task*, and Jagua Nana, the prostitute who has a tremendous following among her colleagues and among the market women because she was at one time trader herself. Jagua Nana is also important because as she travels about looking for fashions she links women across the frontiers. Women, incidentally, are seen in African literature as already on the way to becoming full participants in society. But the writers, particularly the women writers, keep pointing out that this will be psychologically upsetting to them. A large number of career women are portrayed in the literature as misfits, and as yet we do not have a career-woman who is also a mother and who fits into modern society. That such a character has not been created may be an indication that the writers feel that the transition has not yet been completed and perhaps is not even foreseeable in the near future. However, they emphatically deny that women in African culture have, historically, been 'slaves'.

Reference was made earlier to the urban proletariat element known as the 'wild ones'. This group is most aptly represented in one of its forms by Dennis and his girl friend in *Jagua Nana*. These are people without a history or a future. One may ask how they are related to social change. A possible answer is that by being free from the traditional stratifications they are thereby open to modern influences. True, they steal and live a hand-to-mouth existence, but they are free agents. Actually, the fact that such a class has emerged at all is a measure of how much 'civilization' the societies have acquired.[21] The impact of the urban proletariat also includes their 'participation' in the political process as hired private armies of parties or individuals. Wole Soyinka touches on this theme in *The Road*. The 'wild ones' beat up politicians and in that way impede the functions of normal party politics. If we accept the Achebe hypothesis – that the urban proletariat is in fact the major social political force, since all other groups are apathetic[22] – and project it into the future, we can see what their impact on the process of social change will be. We may witness an increasing political chaos and military *coups d'état* which will then be justified in terms of the need to preserve law and order.

The writers do not perceive politicians and the civil servants as a group particularly active in social change in the period prior to independence. The latter are seen as having been effectively muzzled by the British tradition of neutrality of the Civil Service. Among the politicians, only a few of them rose to national recognition and these are lauded by the writers. Jomo Kenyatta is portrayed as being regarded as a Black Moses by most of the people in Ngugi's three novels.[23] Njoka Maki and the Old Man towered above the population in Kachigwe's *No Easy Task*. However, as clearly indicated in Chapter 6, most of the politicians are viewed by the writers as corrupt, self-seeking individuals who become politicians mainly for reasons of self-aggrandisement. Hence they are not thinking individuals. When public officials lose the confidence of the people, the writers seem to tell us, we can infer that they themselves have lost faith in the governing process and thus will impair any social change emanating from it. It is a dismal conclusion in African writing that the masses no longer have faith in the process of government.

The question arises as to what the writers see as necessities for social change in the future. There seem to be four requisites. First is the need to end the system of dominance by politics and politicians. This will make feasible the end of corruption in government. Second, economic acquisition as a monopoly of the politicians must be terminated so that other groups can begin to benefit from independence. Third, government must be made responsive to the wishes of the people through the institution of a meaningful political process based on participation. Finally, by some means, apathy on the part of the people and the attitude that government is something remote and beyond their control must be overcome. Perhaps this can be achieved only through a relinquishing of the habit of the extended family, a salient characteristic of which is the reliance on family patronage. If tradition can be broken in this respect, educated and upcoming men and women will be freed to create and to invest, without fear of the giant family always waiting to be supported. Then they will be able to return to their families rather than hide away in the cities, ending the pejorative term black-white man, i.e., an African who lives like a white man – alone!

One is surprised by the high degree of preoccupation among African writers with defining personal and societal (cultural) identity in terms of Europe. It is true that colonisation broke down African cultures. Yet since the Second World War the accent of the literature has still been on the quest for identity vis-à-vis Europe. This may well be dangerous in the long run. African writers as critics of their own societies may be so preoccupied with 'when the rain began to beat us' that they fail to point out what is wrong today and what the future possibilities are. It was noted earlier that the bureaucrat-intellectual does not stand up to the co-option of the politician. This may explain why the writers do not underscore their criticism of what is wrong with the present order. They are part and parcel of the system, lending 'pith to hollow reeds'. Thus it may be argued that the future must present a clearer role for the literati, as distinct from the politician, or else Africans will always have to say:

> And here we stand
> Lonely and dry.[24]

thereby denying our *weusi*.

Notes

FOREWORD

1. W. E. Abraham, *The Mind of Africa* (Chicago: University of Chicago Press, 1962).

2. Cheikh Anta Diop, *The Cultural Unity of Negro Africa* (Paris: Présence Africaine, 1962).

3. Lewis Nkosi, 'South Africa: Protest', *Africa Report*, VII No. 9 (October 1962) 3–6. Ezekiel Mphahlele, *The African Image* (New York: Praeger, 1962) pp. 2, 6–8; *African Writing Today* (Baltimore: Penguin, 1967) p. 12.

4. New York: Praeger, 1965.

5. New York: Frederick Ungar Publishing Co., 1967.

6. Evanston: Northwestern University Press, 1965.

7. New York: Johnson Reprint Corporation, 1967.

8. New York: Johnson Reprint Corporation, 1967.

CHAPTER 1

1. Joseph Blotner, *The Political Novel* (Garden City: Doubleday and Co., 1955) p. 7.

2. Ibid.

3. *New York Times*, 26 April 1958, p. 17.

4. Leo Lowenthal, *Literature and the Image of Man* (Boston: Beacon Press, 1957) p. 3.

5. George Orwell, *A Collection of Essays* (Garden City: Doubleday and Co., 1957) p. 316.

6. Clive H. Wake, 'African Literary Criticism', *Comparative Literature Studies*, I (1964) 197–8.

CHAPTER 2

1. Roy Sieber, 'Masks as Agents of Social Control', *African Studies Bulletin*, I No. 2 (1962) 8.

2. Austin J. Shelton, 'Behaviour and Cultural Values in West African Stories: Literary Sources for the Study of Culture Contact', *Africa*, XXXIV (1964) 353.

3. Mugo Gatheru, *Child of Two Worlds* (New York: Praeger, 1964).

4. Michael Dei-Anang, *Wayward Lines from Africa* (London and Redhill: Lutterworth Press, 1946) p. 9.

5. Chinua Achebe, 'The Role of the Writer in a New Nation', *Nigeria Maga-zine*, LXXXI (1964) 157.

6. Chinua Achebe, 'The Novelist as Teacher', *New Statesman*, XXIX (January 1965) 161–2.

7. Chinua Achebe, 'The Role of the Writer in A New Nation', *Nigeria Maga-zine*, LXXXI (1964) 158.

8. Oxford University Press, 1965 and Cambridge University Press, 1965, respectively.

9. Chinua Achebe, 'The Black Writer's Burden', *Présence Africaine* (English Ed.), XXXI No. 59 (1956) 138.

10. James Ngugi (Editorial), *East African Journal*, IV No. 1 (January 1968) 3.

11. Wole Soyinka, 'The Writer in the African State', *Transition*, No. 31 (1967) p. 13.

CHAPTER 3

1. 'Literati' is used here to include the artists, the intellectuals and com-mentators who are distinctly not in the government. It is true that some of the artists and intellectuals are in government but analytically the distinction enables us to classify those who are not in the formal bureaucracy.

2. Ulli Beier, 'In Search of African Personality', *Twentieth Century*, CLXV No. 986 (April 1959) 345.

3. Albert Kayper Mensah, 'The Ghosts', in *A Book of African Verse* ed. John Reed and Clive Wake (Heinemann, 1964), pp. 40–1.

4. Nkem Nwankwo, 'Caliban to Miranda', *Ibadan*, No. 21 (October 1964) p. 17.

5. Raynond Sarif Easmon, *The New Patriots: A Play* (Longmans, 1965) p. 33.

6. Chinua Achebe, *A Man of the People* (Heinemann, 1966) pp. 122–3.

7. Ibid., p. 142.

8. Cyprian Ekwensi, *Jagua Nana* (Hutchinson, 1963) p. 137.

9. William Conton, *The African* (New York: New American Libraries, Signet Books, 1961) p. 101.

10. Chinua Achebe, *No Longer at Ease* (Heinemann, 1960) p. 32.

11. Ibid., p. 98.

12. Wole Soyinka, *The Interpreters* (Andre Deutsch, 1965) pp. 119–20.

13. George Awoonor-Williams, 'Exiles', *Black Orpheus*, No. 13 (1963) p. 53.

14. O. G. Nwanodi, *Icheke and Other Poems* (Ibadan: Mbari, 1964) pp. 28–9.

15. T. C. Nwosu, 'The Unbeliever', *Nigeria Magazine*, LXXXI (June 1964) 148.

16. Sagoe believes in the philosophy of 'voidancy' and Sekoni always mut-ters about the primacy of the 'universal dome'. We are never told exactly what the philosophies are.

17. O. G. Nwanodi, *Icheke and Other Poems* (Ibadan: Mbari, 1964) p. 6.

18. Onitsha: Tabansi Bookshop, 1947.

19. Oxford University Press, 1963.

20. Achebe, *A Man of the People*, pp. 3–4.

21. Harvill, 1965.

22. Soyinka, *The Interpreters*, pp. 143–8.

23. Andre Deutsch, 1964.

24. Ibid., p. 25.

25. Ibid., pp. 47–8.

26. Ibid., p. 104.

27. T.C. Nwosu, 'B.B.', *Ibadan*, No. 24 (June 1967) p. 40.

28. Mensah, 'The Ghosts', *A Book of African Verse*, p. 40.

CHAPTER 4

1. Achebe, *A Man of the People*, p. 47.

2. T. M. Aluko, *One Man, One Matchet* (Heinemann, 1964) p. 8.

3. David Rubadiri, *No Bride Price* (Nairobi: East African Publishing House, 1967) pp. 16–17.

4. Soyinka, *The Interpreters*, pp. 27–8.

5. Ibid., passim.

6. T. M. Aluko, *One Man, One Wife* (Heinemann, 1967) p. 38.

7. Ibid., p. 38.

8. Ibid., p. 153.

9. Aluko, *One Man, One Matchet*, passim.

10. T. M. Aluko, *Kinsman and Foreman* (Heinemann, 1966). See also Chief Izongo's Advisor who is B.A., M.A., Ph.D. in Gabriel Okara's *The Voice* (Andre Deutsch, 1964).

11. Aluko, *One Man, One Matchet*, pp. 187–8.

12. Ibid., pp. 193–4.

13. Ibid., p. 196.

14. Lenrie Peters, *The Second Round* (Heinemann, 1965) passim.

15. Rubadiri, *No Bride Price*, passim.

16. Ibid., pp. 93–4.

17. Cyprian Ekwensi, *Iska* (Hutchinson, 1966) passim.

18. R. Sarif Easmon, *The New Patriots*, p. 33.

19. Chinua Achebe, *No Longer at Ease* (New York: Obolensky, 1961) pp. 1–5, passim.

20. Achebe, *A Man of the People*, p. 165.

21. Rubadiri, *No Bride Price*, p. 46.

22. Ibid., pp. 167–9.

23. Ibid., p. 156.

CHAPTER 5

1. Wole Soyinka, *Konoi's Harvest* (Oxford University Press, 1967) p. 1.

2. William Conton, *The African* (New York: New American Library, Signet Books, 1964) p. 178.

3. Obi Egbuna, *Wind Versus Polygamy* (Faber and Faber, 1964) p. 38.

4. Ekwensi, *Jagua Nana*, p. 137.

5. Easmon, *The New Patriots*, p. 2.

6. Achebe, *A Man of the People*, p. 42.

7. Ekwensi, *Jagua Nana*, p. 138.

8. Ibid., p. 142.

9. Easmon, *The New Patriots*, p. 25.

10. Soyinka, *The Interpreters*, pp. 78–9.

11. Achebe, *A Man of the People*, p. 8.

12. Ibid., p. 13.

13. Ibid., p. 128.

14. James Ngugi, *A Grain of Wheat* (Heinemann, 1967), p. 13.

15. James Ene Henshaw, *Medicine for Love* (University of London Press, 1964) p. 43.

16. Ibid., pp. 44–6.

17. Oko p'Bitek, *Song of Lawino* (Nairobi: East African Publishing House, 1967) p. 181.

18. Ibid., pp. 182–3.

19. Ibid., p. 190.

20. A praise song is a traditional Acoli art form. It was sung in praise of the brave or those who distinguished themselves. In this case the praise is for the traditional Acoli things and lament for the modern man.

21. Soyinka, *Kongi's Harvest*, passim; *The Road*, passim; Henshaw, *Medicine for Love*, passim; Ekwensi, *Beautiful Feathers*, passim.

22. Wilson K. Mativo, 'Our True Speaker', *East African Journal* (January 1968) p. 52.

23. Achebe, *A Man of the People*, p. 162.

24. Ibid., p. 108.

25. Ibid., pp. 161–2.

26. p'Bitek, *Song of Lawino*, p. 193.

27. R. E. G. Armattoe, *Deep Down the Black Man's Mind* (Ilfracombe: Stockwell, 1954) p. 23.

28. Ibid., p. 101.

29. Soyinka, *Kongi's Harvest*, pp. 20, 22–4.

30. Ekwensi, *Beautiful Feathers*, p. 78. Italics mine.

31. Wilson K. Mativo, 'Our True Speaker', *East African Journal* (January 1968) pp. 49–52.

32. Aubrey Kachigwe, *No Easy Task* (Heinemann, 1965) p. 88.

33. Ngugi, *A Grain of Wheat*, pp. 191–2.

34. George Awoonor-Williams, 'We Have Found a New Land', *Rediscovery and Other Poems* (Ibadan: Mbari, 1964) p. 10.

35. Achebe, *A Man of the People*, p. 167.

CHAPTER 6

1. Rubadiri, *No Bride Price*, p. 13.

2. Soyinka, *The Interpreters*, pp. 50, 51, 54, 56.

3. Ibid., pp. 241–4.

4. Ekwensi, *Jagua Nana*, p. 167. There is another catechist portrayed in Joseph Wilfred Abruguah, *The Catechist* (Allen and Unwin, 1965).

5. N. U. Akpan, *Ini Abasi and the Sacred Ram* (Longmans, 1966) p. 6.

6. Ekwensi, *Jagua Nana*, passim.

7. Okot p'Bitek, *Song of Lawino. A Lament* (Nairobi: East African Publishing House, 1966) pp 16–17.

8. Ibid., p. 22.

9. Ibid., p. 29.

10. Ibid., p. 48.

11. Ibid., p. 37.

12. Ibid., pp. 99–100.

13. Ibid., p. 41.

14. Ibid., p. 98.

15. Ibid., p. 113.

16. Ibid., p. 116. Italics his.

17. Ibid., pp. 136–42.

18. Ibid., pp. 179–93.

19. Ibid., pp. 194–6.

20. Ibid., pp. 204–5.

21. Joseph W. Abruguah, *The Catechist* (Allen and Unwin, 1965) p. 65.

22. Flora Nwapa, *Efuru* (Heinemann, 1966) p. 281.

23. John Munonye, *The Only Son* (Heinemann, 1966) passim.

24. Ekwensi, *Iska*, p. 96.

25. Ibid., p. 92.

26. Accra: Anowuo Education Publications, 1966, passim.

27. Soyinka, *The Interpreters*, pp. 37–8.

28. Grace Ogot, 'Elizabeth', *East African Journal* (September 1966) pp. 11–18.

29. Ekwensi, *Iska*, passim.

30. D. Olu Olagoke, *The Incorruptible Judge* (Evans Brothers, 1962) p. 28.

31. Abioseh Nicol, *The Truly Married Woman and Other Stories* (Oxford University Press, 1965) p. 12.

32. James Ngugi, *The River Between* (Heinemann, 1965) p. 18.

33. Ogot, *The Promised Land*, passim.

34. Achebe, *Things Fall Apart*, p. 21.

35. Elechi Amadi, *The Concubine* (Heinemann, 1966) passim.

36. Soyinka, *A Dance of the Forests*, pp. 5, 6.

37. Ibid., p. 65.

38. Ogot, *The Promised Land*, passim; Barbara Kimenye, *Kalasanda* (Oxford University Press, 1965).

39. Okara, *The Voice*, passim.

40. Soyinka, *Kongi's Harvest*, p. 77.

41. Ibid., p. 81.

42. Aubrey Kachingwe, *No Easy Task*, pp. 79–83, passim.

43. Achebe, *A Man of the People*, p. 160.

44. Achebe, *A Man of the People*, p. 160.

45. Ibid., p. 166.

46. Francis Selormey, *The Narrow Path* (Heinemann, 1966) p. 5.

47. Obi B. Egbuna, *Wind Versus Polygamy* (Faber, 1964) p. 66.

48. Ibid., p. 67.

49. Ibid., p. 68.

50. Ibid., pp. 68–9.

51. Ibid., p. 70.
52. Ibid., p. 71.
53. Ibid., p. 73.
54. Aluko, *One Man One Wife*, p. 128.
55. Egbuna, *Wind Versus Polygamy.*, pp. 98–9.
56. Onuora Nzekwu, *Highlife for Lizards* (Hutchinson, 1965) p. 46.
57. Ibid., pp. 95–6.
58. Ibid., pp. 130–45.
59. Ibid., pp. 136–7.
60. Ibid., pp. 151–72.
61. Ibid., p. 173.
62. Ibid., p. 173.
63. Ibid., pp. 177–9.
64. Ibid., p. 180.
65. Ibid., p. 192.

CHAPTER 7

1. James Ene Henshaw, *Medicine for Love* (University of London Press, 1964) p. 7. See also Kachingewe, *No Easy Task*, pp. 89–90.
2. Ibid., p. 13.
3. Nkem Nwanko, *Danda* (Andre Deutsch, 1964) passim.
4. J. P. Clark, *Ozidi* (Oxford University Press, 1966) p. 4.
5. James Ngugi, *Weep Not Child* (Heinemann, 1964) p. 57.
6. Rubadiri, *No Bride Price*, pp. 129–30.
7. Cyprian Ekwensi, *Beautiful Feathers* (Hutchinson, 1963) p. 102.
8. Achebe, *No Longer at Ease*, p. 32.
9. Wole Soyinka, *Three Plays* (Ibadan: Mbari, 1963) p. 91.
10. London: Longmans, 1967.
11. Rubadiri, *No Bride Price*, passim.
12. Ekwensi, *When Love Whispers*, passim.
13. Ekwensi, *Beautiful Feathers*, p. 103.
14. Ekwensi, *Jagua Nana*, p. 72.
15. Ibid., p. 124.
16. Ibid., p. 102.
17. Ibid., p. 6.
18. Cyprian Ekwensi, *People of the City* (Dakers, 1954) p. 86.
19. Ibid., p. 15.
20. Ibid., p. 30.
21. Ibid., p. 96.
22. Soyinka, *The Swamp Dwellers,* in *Three Plays*, p. 32. See also Okot p'Bitek, *Song of Lawino*, pp. 195–6.
23. Soyinka, *Three Plays*, pp. 33–4.
24. Ibid.
25. Ibid., p. 40.
26. Ibid., p. 42.
27. Cameron Duodu, *The Gab Boys* (Andre Deutsch, 1967) p. 27.
28. N. U. Akpan, *The Wooden Gong* (Longmans, 1965) p. 2.

29. *The Trials of Brother Jero* in Wole Soyinka, *Three Plays*, p. 56. See also Cyprian Ekwensi, *Iska*, p. 55.

30. Soyinka, *Three Plays*, p. 64.

31. Soyinka, *The Interpreters,* pp. 164–82. See also Aluko, *Kinsman and Foreman*, passim.

32. Soyinka, *The Interpreters*, p. 179.

33. George Awoonor-Williams, *Rediscovery and Other Poems* (Ibadan: Mbari, 1964) p. 11.

CHAPTER 8

1. J. P. Clark, *Agbor Dancer, Poems* (Ibadan: Mbari, 1962) p. 12.

2. James Ene Henshaw, *Children of the Goddess and Other Plays* (University of London Press, 1964) p. 83.

3. Ibid., p. 19.

4. Ibid., p. 29.

5. Ekwensi, Iska, p. 21. See also Selormey, *The Narrow Path*, p. 5 and Ngugi, *The River Between*, pp. 161–75.

6. Selormey, *The Narrow Path*, p. 6.

7. Austin J. Shelton, 'Behavior and Cultural Value in West African Stories', *Literary Sources for the Study of Culture Contract, Africa*, XXXIV (1964) 358.

8. Ekwensi, *Beautiful Feathers*, p. 28. See also T. C. Nwosu, 'BB', *Ibadan*, No. 24 (June 1967) p. 40.

9. Aluko, One Man, One Matchet, p. 185.

10. Peter Lanham and A. Mopeli-Paulus, *Blanket Boys Moon* (Collins, 1953) pp. 301–4; A. Mopeli-Paulus, *Turn to the Park* (Cape, 1956) passim.

11. Soyinka, *The Interpreters*, pp. 241–4.

12. Ogot, *The Promised Land*, pp. 184–94.

13. Chinua Achebe, *Arrow of God* (Heinemann, 1964) p. 287.

14. Chinua Achebe, *Things Fall Apart* (New York: Obolensky, 1959) p. 63. See also Soyinka, *The Strong Breed*, passim.

15. Achebe, *Things Fall Apart*, p. 129.

16. Conton, *The African*, p. 25.

17. Nwanko, *Danda*, passim, pp. 170–1 particularly.

18. E. Latunde Odeku, 'Wandering Lines IV', *Twilight Out of the Night* (Ibadan: University of Ibadan Press, 1964) p. 79.

15. Wilson K. Mativo, 'Our True Speaker', *East African Journal* (January 1968) pp. 49–52.

20. Ekwensi, *When Love Whispers*, passim.

21. Kayira, *The Looming Shadow*, passim.

22. Rubadiri, *No Bride Price*, passim, particularly pp. 125–7.

23. Chinua Achebe, *No Longer at Ease*, passim, especially pp. 31–2 and 83–98.

24. Soyinka, *The Interpreters*, pp. 119–20.

25. Ibid., p. 120.

26. Ibid., pp. 120–1.

27. Ibid., p. 9.

28. Ibid., pp. 11–12. Emphasis mine.

29. Ibid., p. 12.

30. The winds of change refer to the beginning of the nationalist movements which culminated in African independence.

31. Onuora Nzekwu, *Blade Among the Boys* (Hutchinson, 1962) passim.

CHAPTER 9

1. Abioseh Nicol, 'The Meaning of Africa', in *A Book of African Verse*, ed. John Reed and Clive Wake (Heinemann, 1964) p. 45.

2. Simon Kihohia, 'There Had Always Been', *East African Journal* (January 1968) p. 41.

3. Chinua Achebe, 'The Role of the Writer in a New Nation', *Nigerian Libraries*, I No. 3 (September 1964) 113.

4. Chinua Achebe, 'The Novelist as Teacher', *New Statesman*, XXIX (January 1965) 162.

5. Lewis Nkosi, 'A Conversation with Chinua Achebe', *Africa Report*, IX No. 7 (July 1964) 19.

6. In conjunction with this point, see the works of Achebe, Aluko, Soyinka, Ngugi, Nzekwu, Abruguah, Awoonor-Williams and p'Bitek.

7. Francis Ernest Kobina Parkes, 'African Heaven', *Songs from the Wilderness* (University of London Press, 1964) p. 26.

8. Raphael Ernest Grail Armattoe, *Deep Down in the Blackman's Mind* (Ilfracombe: Stockwell, 1954) p. 14.

9. Peggy Rutherford, *Darkness and Light: An Anthology of Native Writing* (Faith Press, 1958) p. 91.

10. Kwesi Brew, 'The Search', *Okyeame*, I (1961) 5.

11. Simon Kihohia, 'There Had Always Been', *East African Journal* (January 1968) p. 41; J. P. Clark argues that they were drugged. See his *Poems*, p. 50.

12. George Awooner-Williams, 'Weaver Bird', *Rediscovery and Other Poems*, p. 16.

13. Stanlake Samkange, *On Trial For My Country* (Heinemann, 1966) p. 6.

14. Ibid., p. 34.

15. Ibid., p. 37.

16. Ibid., p. 53.

17. Ibid., p. 83.

18. Michael Francis Dei-Anang, *Wayward Lines From Africa* (London and Redhill: Lutterworth Press, 1946) p. 27.

19. Clark, *Poems*, p. 44.

20. Ibid., p. 46.

21. Ibid., p. 46.

22. Quoted by John Ferguson, 'Nigerian Poetry in English', *English* XV No. 90 (Autumn 1965) pp. 232–3.

23. Nzekwu, *Blade Among the Boys*, p. 87.

24. Ngugi, *Weep Not Child*, p. 55.

25. Ibid., p. 49.

26. Ibid., pp. 55–6.

27. Joseph Wilfred Abruquah, *The Catechist* (Allen and Unwin, 1965) p. 149.

28. Ngugi, *Weep Not Child*, p. 30.

29. Dennis Chikude Osadebay, *Africa Sings* (Ilfracombe: Stockwell, 1952) p. 10.

30. Ibid., p. 11.

31. E. Latunde Odeku, *Twilight Out of the Night* (Ibadan: University of Ibadan Press, 1964) p. 39.

32. Osadebay, *Africa Sings*, p. 12.

33. Ibid., p. 43.

34. Francis Ernest Kobina Parkes, *Songs From the Wilderness* (University of London Press, 1965) pp. 29, 32–3.

35. Achebe, *No Longer At Ease*, p. 3.

36. David Rubadiri, *Come To Tea* (n.d.) pp. 5–6. Mimeographed.

37. Ngugi, *A Grain of Wheat*, p. 188.

38. Michael Francis Dei-Anang, *Wayward Lines From Africa* (London and Redhill: Lutterworth Press, 1946) p. 7.

39. Ekwensi, *Beautiful Feathers*, p. 62.

40. Lenrie Peters, *Satellites* (Heinemann, 1967) pp. 81, 82, 83, 85.

41. Parkes, *Songs From the Wilderness*, p. 19.

42. Lenrie Peters, *Poems* (Ibadan: Mbari, 1964) p. 14.

43. Obi B. Egbuna, *The Anthill* (Oxford University Press, 1965) pp. 10–11.

44. John Press (ed.), *Commonwealth Literature* (Heinemann, 1965) p. 154.

45. Albert Kayper Mensah, 'The Ghosts', quoted in *A Book of African Verse*, ed. John Reed and Clive Wake (Heinemann, 1964) pp. 39–40.

46. K. A. B. Jones-Quartey, 'Stranger, Why Do You Wonder So', *Okyeane*, I (1961) 22.

47. J. P. Clark, *A Reed in the Tide* (Longmans, 1965) p. 20.

48. Dei-Anang, *Wayward Lines From Africa*, pp. 24–5 (emphasis his).

49. Parkes, *Songs From the Wilderness*, pp. 22–3.

50. George Awoonor-Williams, 'Consummation', *Black Orpheus*, No. 13 (November 1963) p. 51.

CHAPTER 10

1. Francis Ademola, *Reflections: Nigerian Prose and Verse* (Lagos: African Universities Press, 1962) p. 65.

2. Akosua Abbs, *Ashanti Boy* (Collins, 1959) pp. 74–5.

3. Being the title of Achebe's novel which deals with the fall of African culture when European culture intruded. Here we mean the continued fall of indigenous cultures under the onslaught of development planning and other 'modernising' ideologies.

4. Okara, *The Voice*, passim.

5. Ogot, *The Promised Land*, passim.

6. Ekwensi, *Jagua Nana*, passim.

7. R. Sarif Easmon, *Dear Parent and Oore* (Oxford University Press, 1964), passim, particularly pp. 92–3.

8. William Conton, *The African* (New York: New American Library, 1960), pp. 73–4.

9. Ibid., pp. 75–7.

10. Ibid., p. 33.

11. Ibid., pp. 161–2.

12. Ibid., p. 170.

13. Ibid., p. 176.

14. Ibid., p. 177.

15. Ibid., pp. 182–91.

16. Ibid., p. 175.

17. Ibid., p. 192.

18. Ekwensi, *Beautiful Feathers,* p. 11 (emphasis mine).

19. Ekwensi, *Beautiful Feathers*, pp. 134–5.

20. Ibid., p. 137.

21. Nkem Nwankwo, 'Caliban to Miranda', *Ibadan*, No. 21 (October 1965) p. 17.

CHAPTER 11

1. This is an Achebe phrase created out of an Ibo proverb implying bad times.

2. Achebe, *Things Fall Apart*, p. 163.

3. Ibid., p. 147. (Emphasis his.)

4. Ibid., p. 164. (Italics mine.)

5. Nzekwu, *Blade Among the Boys*, p. 87.

6. Chinua Achebe, *Arrow of God* (Heinemann, 1964) p. 51.

7. Ngugi, *The River Between*, p. 24.

8. Conton, *The African*, p. 3.

9. Abruquah, *The Catechist*, p. 20.

10. Munonye, *The Only Son*, passim.

11. Abruquah, *The Catechist*, passim.

12. Nzekwu, *Highlife for Lizards*, p. 167.

13. Ibid., p. 171.

14. Ngugi, *Weep Not Child*, passim.

15. Attwell Sidwell Mopeli-Paulus and Peter Lanham, *Blanket Boy* (New York: Crowell, 1953), passim. and Attwell Sidwell Mopeli-Paulus, *Turn to the Dark* (Cape, 1956) passim.

16. Cyprian Ekwensi, *Passport of Mallam Ilia* (Cambridge University Press, 1960) passim.

17. Ngugi, *Weep Not Child*, p. 30. (Italics his.)

18. Ngugi, *A Grain of Wheat*, p. 25 and passim.

19. Kachigwe, *No Easy Task*, pp. 189–90.

20. Ibid., pp. 175–7.

21. Ekwensi, *Jagua Nana*, p. 128.

22. Achebe, *A Man of the People*, passim.

23. *A Grain of Wheat, The River Between,* and *Weep Not Child*.

24. Okogbule Glory Nwanodi, *Icheke and Other Poems* (Ibadan: Mbari, 1965) p. 12.

Select Biographies

Abbs, Akosua. She is from Ghana.

Aboderin, S. F. He was born about 1928 in Nigeria. He studied Social Sciences in England and returned to teach in the Social Welfare Department at Ibadan. His poetry has been anthologised.

Abruquah, Joseph Wilfred. He is from Ghana.

Achebe, Chinua. He was born in 1930 at Ogidi, Nigeria. He was educated at Government College, Umuahia and University College, Ibadan. He worked for the Nigeria Broadcasting Corporation since 1954 as a producer, and later as the Director of External Broadcasting for the Voice of Nigeria. During the Civil War he was on the Biafran side. Since then he has taught and published in East Central State, Nigeria. His stories have appeared in *Rotarian, Black Orpheus*, and other publications. His novels are widely read in Africa and overseas.

Adali-Morty, Geormbeeyi. He was born in 1916 at Bgledee in Ghana. He was educated at the Roman Catholic Schools at Kpandu and Achimota. He taught for nine years, then in 1946 became a social worker. Later he studied at Cornell University. He was a founder of Okyeame, the literary publication of the Ghana Society of Writers. His poetry has been anthologised.

Addo, Joyce. She was born in 1932 at Sekondi, Ghana and was educated at Achimota. She worked in the Government Statistician's Office from 1951 to 1955. Since then she has worked on broadcasting materials for the Broadcasting Department. Her radio plays have been anthologised.

Adebayo, Yejide. He is from Nigeria.

Adeyemo, G. A. He is from Nigeria. His poetry has been anthologised.

Agbadja, Adolph Kwesi Afordoanyi. He was born in 1928 at Dzodze, Ghana and was educated at the Roman Catholic Mission in Peki Blengo and the Nsawam Methodist School, where he obtained the Primary School Leaving Certificate in 1944. He later took correspondence courses in writing. He joined Radio Ghana in 1956. His stories have been broadcast and anthologised.

Agunwa, Clement. He was born at Ukunu, Gaulu in Nigeria in 1933. He was educated at Ibadan University College and later read for a Diploma in teaching English at Edinburgh University. By 1967 he was Principal of Agulu Grammar School.

Aidoo, Christina Ama Ata. She was born in Ghana and studied at the University of Ghana, Legon. She has been Research Fellow at the Institute of African Studies, University of Ghana, Accra and is currently teaching Literature at the University of Cape Coast, Ghana.

Aig-Imoukhuede, Frank Abiodun. He was born near Ife in Nigeria in 1935 and studied English at the University College at Ibadan, Nigeria. After leaving college he was a radio journalist and later a reporter for the *Daily Express* (Lagos). He later joined the staff of the Ministry of Information, Ibadan. His poetry has been anthologised extensively.

Aiyegbusi, Tunde. He is a Nigerian. He attended Ibadan Boy's High School and Government College, Ibadan, and later Makerere University College in Uganda where he read English. His poetry has been anthologised.

Ajose, Audrey. He is from Nigeria.

Akinsemoyin, Kunle. He was born in Nigeria.

Akobo, B. He is from Nigeria. His poetry has been anthologised.

Akpabot, Samuel. He was born at Uyo, Nigeria. He attended King's College, Lagos, then worked as a sports sub-editor of the *Lagos Daily Times*, and later as a Broadcasting Officer in the Nigerian Broadcasting Corporation. In 1953 he went to England to study music at the Royal College of Music.

Akpan, Ntieyong Udo. He is from Nigeria.

Akpoyoware, Mac. He is from Nigeria. His poetry has been anthologised.

Aluko, T. M. He was born in 1918 at Ilesha, Nigeria. He was educated at Government College, Lagos, and London, where he studied civil engineering and town planning. In 1960 he was appointed Director of Public Works for Western Nigeria, where he stayed for several years before joining the staff of the University of Nigeria, Lagos. His stories have been published by *West African Review*.

Amadi, Elechi. He was born in the village of Allua, near Port Harcourt in Nigeria in 1934. He was educated at Government College, Umuahia, and University College, Ibadan, where he took a degree in Mathematics and Physics. He at one time was a surveyor and later a teacher. He joined the Nigerian army and by 1966 was a captain attached to the Military School at Zaria.

Aniebo, I. N. C. He is from Nigeria. His stories have appeared in *Nigeria Magazine* and *Black Orpheus*.

Annan, Kwabena. He is from Ghana. His short stories have been anthologised.

Apronti, Jawa. He was born in Ghana and educated locally, and later studied at the University of Leeds. His poetry has appeared in *Transition*.

Archibald-Aikins, Samuel. He was born in 1932 in Ghana and educated at the Methodist Senior Boy's School at Cape Coast. He has worked as a clerk in the Ghana Broadcasting System. His poetry has been anthologised.

Arkhurst, Fredericks. He is from Ghana. He was educated at Aberdeen University. He has served as a Ghana diplomat to the United Nations, in the position of First Secretary. He has done army training in Australia and worked for the United Nations Economic Commission for Africa. His poetry has appeared in anthologies.

Armah, Ayi Kwei. He was born in 1939 in Takoradi, Ghana. He was educated at Achimota School in Ghana, Groton School in Massachusetts and Harvard University where he obtained a B.A. in Social Studies. He has worked as a French–English translator in Algiers, a scriptwriter for Ghana television, and an English teacher in Ghana. He has been a translator–editor on the staff of *Jeune Afrique* in Paris. Armah now lives in Tanzania and writes most of the time.

Asalache, Khadambi. He was born in Kenya and was educated locally and in Britain. His poems have appeared in British reviews and *Transition*.

Atarrah, Christina. She is from Sierra Leone. In 1963 she was a secondary school student.

Awooner-Williams, George [Kofi Awoonor]. He was born in 1935 at Keta in the Volta region of Ghana. He studied at Achimota and the University of Ghana at Accra. He has taught at the said University's Institute of African Studies. He worked for a period for the Ghana Film Industry Corporation and has been in the Ghana Diplomatic Service in London. His poetry has been anthologised extensively. At the moment he is teaching literature in an American University.

Babalola, Adeboye. He was born in Nigeria. He studied at Cambridge University and returned to Nigeria where for a time he taught English at Igbobi College in Lagos. His poetry has been anthologised.

Bedwei, Ato. He is from Ghana. His stories have been anthologised.

p'Bitek, Okot. He was born in Uganda. He has worked with the Department of Extramural Studies of Makerere University College and the University of Nairobi. He has been Chairman of the Board of Trustees of the National Theatre of Uganda. His essays and books have been published extensively in English, German and other European languages. At the moment he is teaching at the University of Nairobi.

Bereng, Masupha. He was born at Rothe, Lesotho, in 1928. During the Second World War he served in the army in the Middle East. After the war he worked as a telephone operator. He has had short stories published in anthologies.

Brew, Kwesi. He was born in 1928 at Cape Coast, Ghana. He studied at the University of Ghana, Accra, and entered the Public Service of Ghana in 1953. He later joined the diplomatic service of his country. His poetry has been anthologised extensively.

Brown, C. Enitan. He was born in Ebute Netta, near Lagos, in 1909. He has worked as a railway technician and as director of the Nigerian School of Railway Technology. He has stories in anthologies.

Buahin, Peter Kwame. He was born in 1931 in the State of Assin Apemanim, Ghana. He was educated at Catholic schools at Posu and Elmira. In 1955 he became a teacher at St John's Day Secondary School at Sekondi. The following year he moved to Accra where he has taught at Odorgonno Secondary School. His poetry has appeared in anthologies and Radio Ghana publications.

Chacha, Tom. He was born in Tanzania and educated at St Peter's, Nairobi, and Kabaa High School in Kenya. In 1960 he went to Makerere University College in Uganda where he read for an Arts degree. His short stories have been anthologised.

Chahihu, Bernard Philemon. He was born in Western Kenya in 1944. He is reading English, History and Government at the University College, Nairobi.

Chijioke, Mark. He is from Nigeria. He studied in Britain, where he participated in the B.B.C. Programme, 'West African Voices'. His poetry has been anthologised.

Clark, John Pepper. He was born in Koagbodo in 1935. He was educated at Government College, Ughelli, and Ibadan University College. He worked as an Information Officer at the Ministry of Information after college and subsequently as a journalist and Research Fellow at the African Studies Programs of Ibadan University and Harvard University. He oscillates between writing and lecturing in English at the University of Ibadan. His poetry has been extensively anthologised.

Conton, William. He was born in 1925 in Bathurst, Gambia. He studied in West Africa and England, receiving a B.A. degree from Durham University. He has been Principal of Government Secondary School in Bo, Sierra Leone. He is now a senior official in the Ministry of Education in Freetown, Sierra Leone. His stories have been anthologised extensively.

Cudjoe, Seth D. He was born in 1910 in Ghana. He studied Medicine at Edinburgh and Glasgow Universities between 1932 and 1939, and practised at Chesham, Ilford and London before returning to Ghana in 1955. He has composed, painted, and written poetry which has been anthologised.

Dadson, I. B. He was born in 1920 at Kintampo, Ghana. He was educated at Mfantsipim School, and joined the Civil Service in 1939 where he specialised in accounting. He has translated *The Merchant of Venice* and *Julius Caesar*. His stories and poems have appeared in anthologies.

DeGraft, Joe C. He is from Ghana and is teaching drama at the University of Nairobi. He has been involved in acting in Ghana and Kenya.

Dei-Anang, Michael Francis. He was born in 1909 in Ghana. He was a senior civil servant in the Ghana Ministry of Foreign Affairs until Nkrumah made him Ambassador Plenipotentiary and Minister Extraordinary in the early sixties.

Derimanu, A. B. He was born in 1918 at Tamale in Ghana. He was educated at Tamale, Bagabaga Ridge and at Achimota where he was trained as a teacher in 1940. For ten years he taught at Kpembe, Tekyiman and Tamale. Between 1950 and 1955 he was a court registrar at Tamale. He joined the Broadcasting Department in 1955. His stories have appeared in anthologies.

Djoleto, S. A. A. He was born in 1929 at Somanya in Ghana. He was educated at Accra, Teshie, Ada and Christiansborg schools in Ghana. He later attended the University College, Ghana, where he read English. He has worked as a reporter and his stories have been anthologised.

Dave Danquah, Mabel. She is from Ghana. She studied in England. She was the first African woman to be elected to the legislature. At one time she was editor of *Accra Evening News* but lately she has been a free-lance writer. Her poetry and short stories have been anthologised.

Duodu, M. Cameron. He was born in 1937 at Asiakwa, Ghana. He was educated at the Presbyterian Primary School, and at the Government Middle School in Kibi. He then studied by correspondence to the college level. He has been a teacher, a newspaper reporter and since 1957 he has worked in the news section of the Ghana Broadcasting System.

Easmon, R. Sarif. He was born in Sierra Leone. He is a medical practitioner and politician in Freetown, Sierra Leone. He has many poems in anthologies.

Echeruo, Michael. He was born in 1937 in Owerri in Nigeria.

He was educated at Port Harcourt and University College, Ibadan, where he read English. He has also attended Cornell University in the United States. He lectures in English at the University of Nigeria, Nsukka. His poetry is anthologised extensively.

Egbuna, Obi B. He is from Nigeria.

Egudu, Romanus. He is from Nigeria. He studied at the University of Nigeria, Nsukka, and Michigan State, United States. He was lecturer in the Nigeria University System at Nsukka before the Civil War.

Ekwensi, Cyprian. He was born in 1921 in Nigeria. He was educated at Government College, Ibadan, Achimota College, Ghana, and the School of Forestry, Nigeria; and later studied Pharmacy at London University. He has been a lecturer in English, Science, Pharmacy and a pharmacist. At one time he was Director of Information Services of the Federation of Nigeria. When the Civil War came to Nigeria he sided with Biafra. His stories are extensively anthologised.

Ekwere, John D. He is from Nigeria. His poetry has been anthologised.

Epelle, Sam. He is from Nigeria. His poetry is in anthologies.

Esan, Yetunde. He is from Nigeria and his poetry has been anthologised.

Eyakuze, Valentine. She is from Tanzania. She attended St Mary's in Tabora, Tanzania, then from 1951–7 she studied Medicine at Makerere University College, Uganda. Afterwards she went to Edinburgh, for further studies. Her stories are anthologised.

Faleti, Adebayo. He is a Nigerian poet with an interest in Nigerian folklore. He has been a scriptwriter on the staff of Nigerian Broadcasting Corporation. His poetry has been anthologised.

Gardiner, Robert Kweku Atta. He was born in 1914 at Kumasi in Ghana. He was educated at Adisadel College, Cape Coast, Ghana and Fourah Bay College, Freetown, Sierra Leone. In 1937 he entered the University of Durham to study economics. Later he studied economics and anthropology at Cambridge University. He worked for the United Nations between 1946 and 1949 as a specialist on Trusteeship affairs. In

1949 he became a lecturer at the University of Ibadan, a position he held until 1953 when he returned to Ghana to act as Director of the Department of Social Welfare and Community Development. Subsequently he has worked in the Ministry of Housing and has been Chairman of the Kumasi College of Technology and also Chairman of the Vernacular Literature Board and since about 1965, has been a member of the U.N. Economic Commision for Africa, Addis Ababa.

Ghartey, Joseph. He was born in 1911 at Cape Coast, Ghana. He was educated at the Government Boys School, Cape Coast, and joined the Civil Service in 1929. Since 1937 he has been in the Broadcasting Service where he has written and produced plays for radio. From 1949 to 1950 he studied linguistics and translation at the London school of Oriental and African Studies. Since 1954 he has been a member of the Editorial Committee of the Vernacular Literature Bureau. His plays and poems have been broadcast and anthologised.

Gatuiria, Joseph. He was born in 1939 at Nyeri, Kenya. He was educated in Kenya at Tumtumu School, 1952–4, and Alliance High School, 1955–8. He attended Makerere University College from 1959–64 where he read Economics. Since 1964 he has worked in the Ministry of Finance. His poetry has been included in several anthologies.

Gecau, James K. He is from Kenya. He is currently reading English at University College, Nairobi.

George, Crispin. He is from Sierra Leone.

Gicogo, Gabriel. He is from Nyeri, Kenya. He went to school in Nyeri before receiving an honours degree in Geography at Makerere University College in 1963. He joined the Kenya Civil Service and works at Embu. His poetry has been included in an anthology.

Hagan, G. R. He was born in 1927 at Cape Coast, Ghana. He was educated at the Methodist School, Cape Coast, and at Mfantsipim, where he took the Cambridge School Certificate. He joined the Civil Service in 1949. After three years he left to study at the University College, Ghana. In 1955 he rejoined the Civil Service. He has written plays and stories which have been anthologised and performed on radio.

Henshaw, James Ene. He was born in 1920, in Nigeria.

Hihetah, Robert Kofi. He is from Ghana. His stories have appeared in *Okyeame.*

Higo, Aig. He is from Nigeria. His poetry has been included in three anthologies.

Hoh, Israel Kafu. He was born in 1912 at Afiadenyigba in Ghana. He was educated at Keta, Akropong and Ho. Between 1933 and 1953 he taught English and worked in school administration. He joined the Civil Service in 1953 and has been an education officer. His poetry and drama have been anthologised and performed on radio.

Hokororo, Anthony M. He is from East Africa. He went to Makerere University College in 1955, and gained his Bachelors of Arts degree in 1959 and a Diploma in Education a year later. He later went to Carlton University, Ottawa, Canada, to pursue graduate studies. He has poems in an anthology.

Horatio-Jones, Edward Babatunde. He is a Nigerian writer and film producer.

Idan, L. K. He was born in 1921 at Winneba, Ghana. He was educated at Methodist School, Winneba, at Adisadel College, Cape Coast, at the School of Art at Achimota, and the College of Technology at Kumasi. He has been a textile designer and arts and crafts teacher. He is the author of plays and poems which have been anthologised.

Ijimere, Obotunde. He was born in 1930 in Nigeria.

Ike, Vincent Chukwuemeka. He was born in 1931 in Nigeria.

Irele, Abiola. He is from Nigeria. He has written literary criticism. His poems have been anthologised.

Johnson, Lemuel. He is from Sierra Leone. His story has appeared in *Journal of the New African Literature and the Arts.*

Jones, Eldred Durosimi. He is from Sierra Leone and his poetry has been anthologised. He has also written literary criticism. He has been Chairman of the English Department at Fourah Bay College, Sierra Leone.

Jones-Quartey, K. B. He is from Ghana. He has studied in the United States. He has been director of Extra-Mural Studies at the University of Ghana.

Kabushenga, Sabiti. He was born in Kabale, Uganda in 1945. A student at Makerere University College, Kampala, his poems have appeared in *Transition*.

Kachingwe, Aubrey. He was born in 1926 in Malawi. He was educated locally and in Tanzania. He worked as a cub journalist in Kenya from 1950 to 1954 before leaving to study journalism at London in 1955. In England he has worked for the *Daily Herald* and the African News Service of the British Broadcasting Service. Before returning to head the News Bureau of Malawi Broadcasting Corporation, he worked for a time with Ghana Broadcasting Corporation.

Kaggwa, Michael. He was born in Uganda and educated at St Mary's College, Kisubi and graduated from Makerere University College with honours in English in 1960. He joined the Uganda Diplomatic Service and has worked in, among other positions, the Uganda High Commissioner's Office in London. His stories and poems are in anthologies.

Kagwe, Solomon. He was born in 1939 in Nyeri, Kenya. He was educated at Makerere University College where he gained a B.A. in English, History and Political Science in 1964. His stories have been included in an anthology.

Kariara, Jonathan. He was born in 1935 in Nyeri, Kenya. After graduating in English from Makerere University College, he worked for seven years with the book production division of the East African Bureau in Nairobi. Since 1966 he has worked as part of the Oxford University Press editorial staff. His short stories and poems are included in anthologies.

Karibo, Minji. He is from Nigeria and has had poems included in anthologies.

Karienye, M. He is from East Africa. He studied History at Makerere University College. He writes a regular column in the *Weekly News* under the name of Karienye Yohanna. His stories and poems have been anthologised.

Kariuki, Joseph E. He was born in Kenya. He was educated at Makerere University College and King's College, Cambridge. He read for a Masters Degree in English and Management. He is presently the Principal of the Kenya Institute of

Administration. His poetry has been extensively anthologised.

Kataka, Awori. He was born in 1944 in Kakamega District in Kenya. He was a student at University College, Nairobi, reading English, History and Political Science. His stories have appeared in *East African Journal*. Awori is a journalist in Nairobi.

Kayira, Legson. He was born in Malawi. He completed his high-school education at a mission school. Subsequently he has studied in the United States at Skagit Valley and the University of Washington, and in England at Cambridge University.

Khamadi, Miriam. She is from Kenya. After finishing her school certificate in 1960 at Butere Girl's School she left the following year for the United States. She attended William Penn College and Indiana University. She returned to Kenya in 1965 and has taken a post-graduate Diploma in Education at Makerere University College. Her poems have appeared in *Transition*.

Khunga, Cuthbert. He is from Malawi. He was educated at Dedza Government Secondary School, and went to Makere University College in Uganda in 1960. By 1963 he had finished his B.A. in English, History and Political Science. He was the first African to become Regional Information Officer before Malawi gained independence. Presently he is in the Malawi Diplomatic Service and has been stationed, among other places, in West Germany. He has had stories included in an anthology.

Kibera, Leonard. He is from Kenya and is a student at the University College, Nairobi. His stories and poetry have appeared in *Transition* and *East African Journal*.

Kohohia, Simon. He is from Nyeri, Kenya. He read International Relations and Economics at Hamline University in the United States.

Kimenye, Barbara. She is from Buganda, Uganda. Before the deposition of the Kabaka Government she worked in the Buganda Civil Service. She is a journalist in Nairobi, Kenya.

Kimura, Joseph H. He was born in Muranga, Kenya in 1946. He is currently studying commerce at the University College, Nairobi.

King, Delphine. She is from Sierra Leone.

Kokunda, Violet. She was born in Ankole, Uganda. She was educated at Bweranyangi and Kyebanbe Schools, and then Gayaze High School. Later she attended Makerere University College where she read History. She has taken part in school broadcasting for Radio Uganda. Her radio plays and stories have been anthologised.

Komey, Ellis Ayitey. He was born in 1927 in Accra, Ghana, and educated at Accra Academy. He has been the African Editor of *Flamingo* in London, where he has lived for a long time. He has edited an anthology of African stories and his poetry has been anthologised extensively.

Konadu, Samuel Asare. He was born in Ashanti, Ghana in 1932. He went to primary and middle school at Abuakwa. In 1951 he joined the Ghana Information Service and worked as a reporter for a series of government papers and the then Gold Coast Broadcasting Service. In 1956 he was awarded a government scholarship to study journalism at Strasbourg University and at London. After two years he returned to Ghana to join the Ghana News Agency which he left in 1963 to devote himself to research in traditional customs and practices, and writing.

Kyei, Kojo Gyinaye. He was born in 1930 at Ahafo, Ghana. He studied at St Augustine's College, Cape Coast, Ghana. Later he studied architecture at the University of Kansas, United States. His poetry has been anthologised.

Kurankyi-Taylor, Dorothy. She is from Ghana.

Laryea, Bossman. He was born in 1910 at Accra, Ghana. He joined the Civil Service in 1930. His short stories have been anthologised and read over the radio.

Lindsay, J. K. O. He was born in 1933 at Cape Coast, Ghana and educated at Mfantsipim School. He was trained as a teacher at Kumasi College of Technology and subsequently read Economics at London University. He writes for British and Ghanaian newspapers as well as Ghana Radio. His stories and radio plays have been anthologised.

Liyong, Taban Lo. He is from Gulu in Uganda and he was educated locally, and at the Iowa Writers' Workshop and at Howard University, Washington, D.C. At present he is on the faculty of the University of Nairobi, teaching Oral Literature.

Markwei, Matei. He is from Sierra Leone. He studied theology in the United States at Lincoln University, and at Yale University. He is an ordained Minister. Presently he is Dean of Students at Freetown Teacher's College.

Martey, E. K. He was born in 1935 at Accra, Ghana. He was educated locally at Africa College. He works in the Medical Research Institute as a laboratory assistant. His articles and poems have appeared in journals and anthologies, as well as being read over Radio Ghana.

Mativo, Wilson K. He was born in Kitui, Kenya in 1945. He is a student at Strathmore College, Nairobi. Essentially he writes stories. His stories have appeared in *East Africa Journal*.

Mbiti, John. Born in Kitui, Kenya. He was educated at Makerere University College, at several institutions in the United States and at Cambridge University where he got his Doctorate in Religion. He lectures on the New Testament and African Traditional Religions at Makerere University College, where he is professor and chairman of the Department of Philosophy and Religion. His poetry has appeared in *Transition* and he has had stories in *Présence Africaine*.

Mbure, Samuel. He is from Kenya and was born in 1950. He did not complete primary school. He has published poems locally and some have been broadcast by the Voice of Kenya.

Menkiti, Ifeanyi. He was born at Onitsha in 1940. He completed a Master of Science Degree in Journalism from Columbia University in 1960. His poems have appeared in *Transition* and other magazines in Nigeria and the United States.

Mensah, Albert W. Kayper. He was born in 1923 at Sekondi in Ghana. He was educated at Mfantsipim School, Ghana. Achimota College, Ghana, Queen's College, Cambridge, and London University. He is a teacher at Wesley College, Kumasi, Ghana. He is the author of many plays and poems which have been broadcast and anthologised.

Mensah, G. M. K. He was born in 1935 at Agbozume-Amukoe, Ghana. He was educated at Government Secondary Technical School at Takoradi. He worked as a farmer, a weaver and a fisherman before joining the Ghana Broadcasting System for in-service training. He has been anthologised.

Mensah, J. U. He was born in 1935 in Elmina, Ghana. He was educated in Catholic Schools in Abosso, Tarkwa and Elmina. He has written for local newspapers and his stories have been anthologised.

Milner, Brown A. L. He is a Ghanaian free-lance writer, newspaper man and teacher in Accra. His poetry has appeared in anthologies.

Mkapa, Ben. He was born in 1938 at Ndanda, Tanzania, and educated at St Francis College, Dar es Salaam, and Makerere University College, as well as at Columbia University where he did graduate work. He has been in the Tanzania Civil Service since 1962. Since 1963 he has been in the Ministry of External Affairs and Defence, rising to Assistant-Secretary. He also has worked as a journalist. His poetry has been anthologised.

Munonye, John. He was born in 1929 in Akokwa, Nigeria. He was educated at Christ the King College, Onitsha, and at University College, Ibadan. He read Latin, Greek and History. He did graduate work at London University. Since 1954 he has worked at the Ministry of Education. In 1966 he was a senior Inspector of Education in Eastern Nigeria.

Mutiga, Joseph G. He was born in 1940 in Kenya. He attended Kagumo Secondary School in Kenya and Makerere University College where he was awarded his B.A. in 1964. He joined the Kenya Civil Service afterwards as an administrative officer. His stories have been anthologised.

Mushanga, Musa. He was born in Kagago in Uganda. After being a medical assistant he studied religion at Makerere University College. His poetry has appeared in *Transition*.

Mwalilino, Katoki. He is from Malawi and his poetry has been anthologised in *Présence Africaine*.

Mwangi, Thomas. He is from Kenya, and is being trained as a teacher at Kenyatta College.

Nagenda, John. He was born in 1938 at Gahini in Rwanda where his father was a missionary from Uganda. He studied English at Makerere University College from 1957–62. He works for Oxford University Press in Nairobi. He has been a radio and magazine critic. His stories and poems have appeared in magazines and anthologised.

Ndlovu, Joshua. He was born in 1937 in Bulawayo, Southern Rhodesia, and educated in South Africa at Marrian Hill, Natal, and University of Natal, Durban. Presently he is a graduate student in Public Administration at Syracuse University in the United States.

Ndumbu, Abu D. He is from Kenya and is working in radio broadcasting.

Ngugi, James. He was born at Limuru, Kenya in 1938. He was educated at Alliance High School in Kenya, at Makerere University College, Uganda, and at the University of Leeds. He studied English. At Makerere he wrote two novels and a play. He has worked in journalism in Kenya. He lectures at the University College, Nairobi. His stories are widely anthologised.

Ngulukulu, N. G. He was born in Pugu, Tanzania. He was educated in the vicinity of Pugu and later at Makerere University College where he graduated with Honours in English in 1964. Afterwards he went to King's College, Cambridge to pursue graduate studies. His poetry has been included in an anthology.

Nicol, Abioseh. He was born in Sierra Leone. He was educated in Nigeria. Later he studied Medicine at London University and Cambridge University. He has written articles extensively in *Encounter, The Times, The Economist, The Guardian, Transition* and *West Africa*. He is the Principal of Fourah Bay College, the University of Sierra Leone. His poetry and stories have been included in ten anthologies.

Njau, Rebecca. She was born in Kikuyu in Kenya. She studied at Makerere University College. In 1960 her first play, *The Scar*, won a drama festival award at the National Theatre in Kampala. Her poetry has been anthologised.

Nketia, J. H. Kwabema. He was born in 1921 at Ashanti Mampong, Ghana. He was educated at Presbyterian schools at Mampong and Akropong between 1928 and 1941. He taught at the Teacher Training College at Akropong for two years before proceeding to study linguistics at London School of Oriental and African studies. He has many books in Twi traditional literature, translations and poetry as well as scholarly anthropological works. He is best known as a musicologist of the Akan peoples. His poems have been anthologised.

Nugi, Paul K. He was born in 1948 in Githuguri, Kenya. He is at Strathmore College, Nairobi.

Nwankwo, Nkem. He was born in 1936 in Nigeria, and is a graduate of the University of Ibadan. His stories and poems are widely anthologised.

Nwanodi, Okogbule Glory. He was born in 1936 at Diobu, Nigeria. He studied English at the University of Nigeria, Nsukka, and the University of Iowa. Before he went to the University of Nigeria at Nsukka he had trained as a teacher and had worked as a schoolmaster.

Nwapa, Flora. She was born in 1931 and grew up in Oguta, Nigeria. She attended school at both Port Harcourt and Lagos. She read for an Arts degree at University College, Ibadan, from 1953 to 1957. The following year she got her Diploma in Education at Edinburgh University. On returning to Nigeria she was an education officer for a period and taught English and geography for a while. Since 1963 she has been at the University of Lagos as an Assistant Registrar in Public Relations.

Nweke, Chuba. He is from Nigeria. He has worked for the London and Kano Trading Company at Lagos. His poetry is included in an anthology.

Nwoga, Donatus Ibe. He was born in 1933 at Ekwarazu, Nigeria. He studied English Literature at Queens University, Belfast and the University College, London. He later got a Ph.D. in West African Literature at the University of London. Before the Civil War he was a lecturer in English and African Literature at the University of Nsukka, Nigeria. His poetry has appeared in many literary magazines.

Nyaku, Frank Kofi. He was born in 1924 at Ho, Ghana. He was educated at Achimota where he graduated as a teacher in 1943. Since 1952 he has been an education officer in the Civil Service. He has composed songs, published school textbooks, written biography and collected an anthology of short stories and poems in Ewe. His stories and poems have been anthologised.

Nzekwu, Onuora. He was born in 1928 at Kafanchan, Nigeria. He was educated locally, completing a teachers' course. He taught for nine years at Oturkpo, Onitsha and Lagos before joining the staff of *Nigeria Magazine* in 1956 as an editorial assistant. He has been Editor of that magazine since 1962.

Obika, Francis. He was born near Ogidi in Nigeria. He was educated in Lagos and at the Yaba School of Pharmacy. After about five years as a government pharmacist, he established his own practice. His poetry has been included in an anthology.

Oculi, Joseph Okello. He is from Uganda. He read Political Science at Makerere University College and did graduate work at the University of Essex. He has published a long poem and a novel. He is finishing a Ph.D programme in political science in America.

Odeku, E. Latunde. He is from Nigeria. He studied Medicine in the United States.

Odhiambo, E. S. Atieno. He is from Kenya and has read history at the University of Nairobi where he is completing his Ph. D. work.

Ofori, Henry. He was born in 1924 at Oda, Ghana. He was educated in Government schools at Sefwi Wiawso and Accra. Later he attended Achimota College, graduating in 1943. He worked at the Royal Air Force Base at Takoradi in 1944 and also for two and a half years as Soil Analyst for the West African Coca Research Institute at Tafo. After attending the University College, Ghana, he taught physics at Takoradi until 1954. In 1955 he joined the staff of the *Daily Graphic* as a columnist and in 1957 became Editor of *Drum* publications. He writes short stories and poetry and has been anthologised.

Ogot, Grace A. She was born in 1930 in Nyanza, Kenya. After high school she trained as a nurse and midwife in Uganda and Britain. She worked as a nurse in Kenya and Uganda and later as a Community Development Officer before working with the B.B.C. Overseas Service as a script-writer and announcer. She is presently Public Relations Officer for Air India in East Africa. Her stories have been anthologised extensively.

Ogunyemi, Wale. He is from Nigeria.

Okafor, Michael. He is from Nigeria. He studied agriculture at the University College, Ibadan.

Okara, Gabriel Imomotimi. He was born in 1921 in the Niger

Delta area of Nigeria. He was educated at Government College, Umuahia, and then became a bookbinder. He wrote plays and features for broadcasting. He has been Information Officer with the Eastern Regional Government at Enugu. His poetry and stories are widely anthologised.

Okigbo, Christopher. He was born near Onitsha in 1932 and studied classics at University College, Ibadan. At one time he was Private Secretary to the Federal Minister of Research and Information, Nigeria. He had also been a member of the Library staff of University of Nigeria at Nsukka and Manager of Cambridge University Press in West Africa. He was a poet, probably the leading poet in Africa. He was widely anthologised. Okigbo died during the Nigerian Civil War in 1967. He had supported the Biafran cause.

Okogie, M. O. He is from Nigeria.

Okonkwo, Nathan N. D. He is from Nigeria.

Okoye, Mokwugo. He was born in 1926 in Nigeria.

Okpaku, Joseph O. O. He is from Nigeria. He studied in the Department of Theatre Arts at Stanford University for his doctorate. He is the Editor of the *Journal of the New African Literature and the Arts* and has set up a publishing house in New York.

Olagoke, D. Olu. He is from Nigeria.

Oleghe, Pious. He is from Nigeria. He has appeared in several poetry anthologies.

Opara, Ralph Chukuemeka. He is from Nigeria and has appeared in two poetry anthologies.

Opoku, Andrew Amankwa. He was born in 1912 in Bechem, Ghana. He was a teacher from 1935 to 1951 when he then became an editor for the Bureau of Ghana Languages. Since 1956 he has been an announcer and literary consultant to Radio Ghana. His poems have been anthologised.

Osadebay, Dennis Chikude. He was born in 1911 at Asaba, Nigeria. He studied law in England. He has been a member of the Federal Parliament and Premier of the Midwestern Region, among other important public offices.

Otoo, S. K. He was born in 1910 at Otuam, Ghana. He was educated at the Wesleyan Methodist Schools at Tantum,

Tarkwa and Saltpond, and at Wesley College at Kumasi. He has been a teacher, Editor of the Vernacular Literature Bureau and a Member of Parliament since 1954. His works have been anthologised.

Owoyele, David. He is from Nigeria and has stories and poetry in anthologies.

Parkes, Francis Kobina. He was born at Korlebu in Ghana, and went to school at Adisadel, Ghana. After some time as a newspaper reporter, since 1955 he has worked for Radio Ghana. His poetry has been anthologised extensively.

Pederek, Simon. He is from Ashanti, Ghana. His poetry has been anthologised.

Peters, Lenrie. He was born at Bathurst, Gambia in 1932. He was educated in Sierra Leone and Cambridge Technical College in England. He later read Natural Sciences at Trinity College, Cambridge. He is a doctor as well as a surgeon. His poetry is extensively anthologised.

Raditladi, L. D. He is from Botswana. He was educated at Mission Schools in Botswana and later in South Africa at Fort Hare University College. He has a story in one anthology.

Rubadiri, David. He was born in Malawi in 1930. He was educated in Makerere University College and Cambridge University. He now teaches English at Makerere University College. He has served in the Diplomatic Service and Ministry of Education of Malawi. His poems have been anthologised.

Segun, Mabel. She is from Nigeria. Her poetry has appeared in anthologies.

Selormey, Francis. He was born in 1927 in Ghana.

Setsoafia, H. K. B. He was born in 1920 at Anloga, Ghana. He studied at the Presbyterian School at Anloga and finished his high school studies by correspondence. He has worked as a store clerk, a teacher and a programme assistant in the Broadcasting Department. His plays have been broadcast and anthologised.

Sey, K. Abaka. He is from Ghana. His work has appeared in *Présence Africaine*.

Sinah, M. W. He was born in 1923 in Sierra Leone. He

attended Roman Catholic schools until 1935. After this period he worked as a teacher until he was drafted into the army during the Second World War. He has worked for an oil company in Freetown since his discharge. He has a story in an anthology.

Smith, J. Aggrey. He was born in 1921 at Cape Coast, Ghana and educated at Government Boy's School, Cape Coast, and Adisadel College. Between 1941 and 1951 he was in the Civil Service in the Customs and Excise Department. In 1951 he obtained his B.A. degree by correspondence. Since 1951 he has been a teacher as well as an ordained Minister. His poetry has been anthologised.

Sofola, Samuel Adeniyi. He is from Nigeria.

Sofowote, Segun. He is from Nigeria.

Soyinka, Wole. He was born at Abeokuta, Nigeria in 1935. He studied English at the University College, Ibadan, and later read for an English Honours degree at Leeds University. He has held teaching and research positions at the Universities of Ife, Ibadan and Lagos. He is a writer of drama, novelist, actor, poet and essayist. He established the Masks – a dramatic company – in 1960. Before he was placed in detention by the Nigerian government in 1967 he had just announced plans for establishing an African–American movie-producing company. He has poems and essays in many publications and anthologies.

Ssemuwanga, John B. K. He was born near Kampala, Uganda in 1941 and is a recent graduate of Makerere University College. His work appeared in student publications while he was at college. He is a poet.

Standa, Everett. He was born in Western Kenya in 1946. He is studying for a B.A. degree at the University College, Nairobi.

Sutherland, Efua Tahodora. She was born in 1924 at Cape Coast, Ghana. She studied teaching at Cambridge University. She and her husband at one time founded and ran a school in the Transvolta section of Ghana. She works with the Drama School of the University of Ghana. Her original plays and adaptations have been broadcast. Her poetry is extensively anthologised.

Tahir, Ibrahim. He is a Nigerian on the staff of B.B.C., London.

Thuo, James. He is from Kenya. He is a trainee teacher at Kenyatta College but aspires to being a full-time writer.

Tutuola, Amos. Born in 1920 at Abeokuta, Nigeria. He had only a primary education at a local school. He was a blacksmith and now works for the Labour Department of Nigeria at Lagos. He has had numerous articles in *Black Orpheus*, and *Présence Africaine*.

Umukoro, Gordon. He is from Nigeria and his poetry has been included in one anthology.

Ukwu, U. I. He is from Nigeria and his poetry has appeared in two anthologies.

Waiguru, Joseph. He was born in 1939 in Nyeri, Kenya. He was educated at Kangaru Secondary School. He attended Makerere University College from 1959–64, graduating in English, Economics, and Political Science. His poetry has been included in an anthology.

Waiyaki, Edwin. He is from Kenya. His poetry has been published in the *East African Journal*.

Wardy, F. K. Chapman. He was born in 1924 at Saltpond, Ghana. He was educated at Saltpond and St Augustine's Roman Catholic College where he passed the Cambridge School Certificate in 1945. The same year he joined the Civil Service, where he works in the Accountant Generals Department. His poetry has been anthologised.

Williams, Gaston Bart. He is from Sierra Leone. His work has appeared in *Black Orpheus*.

Winful, E. Archie. He was born in 1922 at Saltpond, Ghana. He was educated at Mfantsipim School and University College of the South-West at Exeter in 1947. He then worked at the London School of Oriental and African Studies and trained as a book editor at Oxford University Press. Since 1949 he has been variously employed as editor, schoolmaster, and officer in the administration. His stories have appeared in anthologies.

Zirimu, Elvania Namukwaya. She was born in 1938 near Entebbe in Uganda. She attended King's College, Budo, Uganda and went on to Makerere University College where she qualified as a teacher. She has subsequently taken an English Honours degree at Leeds University. Her stories and poems have appeared in several magazines and in an anthology. At the moment she works in radio broadcasting and local drama.

Bibliography

PRIMARY SOURCES

Anthologies

Ademola, Frances (ed.). *Reflections: Nigerian Prose and Verse.* Lagos: African Universities Press, 1962.

Banham, Martin J. (ed.). *Nigerian Student Verse.* Ibadan: Ibadan University Press, 1960.

Bassir, Olumbe (ed.). *An Anthology of West African Verse.* Ibadan: Ibadan University Press, 1957.

Beier, Ulli (ed.). *Black Orpheus: An Anthology of New African and Afro-American Stories.* New York: 1957.

Cook, David (ed.). *Origin East Africa.* Heinemann, 1965.

Denny, Neville (ed.). *Pan-African Short Stories.* Nelson, 1965.

Drachler, Jacob (ed.). *African Heritage: Intimate Views of the Black Africans from Life, Lore and Literature.* New York: Crowell-Collier, 1963.

Edwards, Paul (ed.). *Modern African Narrative.* Nelson, 1966.
Through African Eyes. 6 vols. Cambridge: Cambridge University Press, 1966.
West African Narrative: An Anthology for Schools. Nelson, 1963.

Hughes, Langston (ed.). *An African Treasury: Articles, Essays, Stories and Poems by Black Africans.* New York: Crown, 1960.

Hughes, Langston (ed.). *Poems from Black Africa.* Bloomington: Indiana University Press, 1963.

Komey, Ellis Ayitheh and Mphahlele, Ezekiel (eds.). *Modern African Stories.* Faber and Faber, 1964.

Moore, Gerald and Beier, Ulli (eds.). *Modern Poetry from Africa.* Baltimore: Penguin, 1963.

Mphahlele, Ezekiel (ed.). *African Writing Today.* Baltimore: Penguin, 1967.

Nwoga, Donatus Ibe (ed.). *West African Verse: An Anthology.*

New York: Humanities Press, 1967.

Reed, John and Wake, Clive (eds.). *A Book of African Verse.* Heinemann, 1964.

Ridout, Ronald and Jones, Eldred (eds.). *Adjustments: An Anthology of African and Western Writing.* Edward Arnold, 1966.

Rive, Richard (ed.). *Modern African Prose.* Heinemann, 1964.

Rutherfoord, Peggy (ed.). *African Voices: An Anthology of Native African Writing.* New York: Vanguard Press, 1960.

Swanzy, Henry. *Voices of Ghana: Literary Contributions to the Ghana Broadcasting System, 1955–7.* Accra: Ministry of Information and Broadcasting, 1958.

Tibble, Anne. *African-English Literature: A Survey and Anthology.* Peter Owen, 1965.

Whiteley, W. H. (ed.). *A Selection of African Prose* (Vol. II, written prose.) Clarendon Press, 1964.

Books

Abbs, Akosua. *Ashanti Boy.* Collins, 1960.

Abruquah, Joseph Wilfred. *The Catechist.* Allen and Unwin, 1965.

Achebe, Chinua. *Arrow of God.* Heinemann, 1964.
    Chike and the River. Cambridge: Cambridge University Press, 1966.
    A Man of the People. Heinemann, 1966.
    No Longer at Ease. New York: Obolensky, 1961.
    The Sacrificial Egg and Other Short Stories. Onitsha: Etudo Ltd., 1962.
    Things Fall Apart. New York: Obolensky, 1959.

Adebayo, Yejide. *Three Plays.* Lagos: Nigeria Printing and Publishing Company, 1957.

Agunwa, Clement. *More Than Once.* Longmans, 1967.

Aidou, Christina Ama Ata. *The Dilemma of a Ghost.* Longmans, 1965.

Ajose, Audrey. *Yomi in Paris.* Cambridge: Cambridge University Press, 1966.

Akinsemoyin, Kunle. *Twilight Tales.* Lagos: African Universities Press, 1966.

Akpabot, Samuel. *Masters of Music.* Ilfracombe: Stockwell, 1958.

Akpan, N. U. *Ini Abasi and the Sacred Ram.* Longmans, 1966.

The Wooden Gong. Longmans, 1965.

Aluko, T. M. *Kinsman and Foreman*. Heinemann, 1966.

One Man, One Matchet. Heinemann, 1964.

One Man, One Wife. Lagos: Nigeria Printing and Publishing Company, 1959.

Amadi, Elechi. *The Concubine*. Heinemann, 1966.

Armattoe, Raphael. *Between the Forest and the Sea: Collected Poems*. Lomeshie Research Centre, 1950.

Deep Down in the Blackman's Mind. Ilfracombe: Stockwell, 1954.

Asalache, Khadambi. *A Calabash of Life*. Longmans, 1967.

Awogbajo, B. S. *Accidents: A Play in Five Parts*. Lagos: Author, 1959.

Awoonor-Williams, George. *Rediscovery and Other Poems*. Ibadan: Mbari, 1964.

Bedioko, Kwabena Asare. *Don't Leave Me*. Accra: Anowuo Educational Publications, 1966.

p'Bitek, Okot. *The Song of Lawino: A Lament*. Nairobi: East African Publishing House, 1967.

Song of Ocol. Nairobi: East African Publishing House, 1968.

Two Songs. Nairobi: East African Publishing House, 1972.

Chidia, Godwin Paul. *Queen of Night*. Port Harcourt: Author, 1957.

Three Plays. Oxford University Press, 1964.

Clark, John Pepper. *Poems*. Ibadan: Mbari, 1962.

A Reed in the Tide. Longmans, 1965.

Song of a Goat. Ibadan: Mbari, 1961.

Conton, William. *The African*. New York: New American Library, 1961.

DeGraft, J. C. *Sons and Daughters*. Oxford University Press, 1964.

Dei-Anang, Michael Francis. *Africa Speaks: A Collection of Original Verse with an Introduction on Poetry in Africa*. Accra: Guinea Press, 1959.

Cocoa Comes to Mampong. Cape Coast: Methodist Book Depot, 1949.

Ghana Semi-tones. Accra: Presbyterian Book Depot, 1962.

Dei-Anang, Michael Francis and Yaw, Warren. *Ghana Glory: Poems on Ghana and Ghanaian Life*. Nelson, 1965.

Dei-Anang, Michael Francis. *Okomfo Anokye's Golden Stool*.

Ilfracombe: Stockwell, 1959.

Two Faces of Africa. Accra: Waterville Publishing House, 1965.

Wayward Lines from Africa. United Society for Christian Literature, 1946.

Duodu, Cameron. *The Gab Boys*. Andre Deutsch, 1967.

Easmon, R. Sarif. *The Burnt Out Marriage*. Nelson, 1967.

Easmon, R. Sarif. *Dear Parent and Ogre*. Oxford University Press, 1964.

The New Patriots. Longmans, 1965.

Egbuna, Obi B. *Wind Versus Polygamy*. Faber, 1964.

The Anthill. Oxford University Press, 1965.

Ekwensi, Cyprian. *An African Night's Entertainment*. Lagos: African Universities Press, 1962.

Beautiful Feathers. Hutchinson, 1963.

The Boa Suitor. Nelson, 1966.

Burning Grass. Heinemann, 1962.

The Drummer Boy. Cambridge: Cambridge University Press, 1960.

The Great Elephant Bird. Nelson, 1965.

Ikolo the Wrestler. Nelson, 1947.

Iska. Hutchinson, 1966.

Jagua Nana. Hutchinson, 1961.

Juju Rock. Lagos: African Universities Press, 1966.

The Leopard's Claw. Longmans, 1950.

Lokotown and Other Stories. Heinemann, 1966.

The Passport of Mallam Ilia. Cambridge: Cambridge University Press, 1960.

People of the City. Dakers, 1954.

The Rainmaker and Other Stories. Lagos: African Universities Press, 1965.

Trouble in Form Six. Cambridge: Cambridge University Press, 1966.

When Love Whispers. Onitsha: Tabansi Bookshop, 1947.

Henshaw, James Ene. *Children of the Goddess and Other Plays*. University of London Press, 1964.

Medicine for Love. University of London Press, 1964.

This is Our Chance. University of London Press, 1956.

Horatio-Jones, Edward Babatunde Bankole. *The Mockers*. Switzerland: Artemis Verlag, 1963.

Ijimere, Obotunde. *The Fall of Man.* Oshogbo: Theatre Express Sketches, 1966.

Ike, Vincent Chukuemeka. *Toads for Supper.* Harvill Press, 1965.

Iwuji, Victoria B. *Going to a Moonlight Play.* Ibadan: African Education Press, 1966.

Kachingwe, Aubrey. *No Easy Task.* Heinemann, 1965.

Kariara, Jonathan. *The Green Bean Patch.* Performed at the Uganda Drama Festival, 1960. Mimeo.

Kayira, Legson. *The Looming Shadow.* Garden City: Doubleday, 1967.

Kibera, Leonard and Kahiga, Samuel. *Potent Ash.* Nairobi: East African Publishing House, 1967.

Kimenye, Barbara. *Kalasanda.* Oxford University Press, 1965.
Kalasanda Revisited. Oxford University Press, 1966.

King, Delphine. *Dreams of Twilight.* Apapa: Nigerian National Press, 1962.

Konadu, Samuel Asare. *Come Back Dora.* Accra: Anowuo Education Publications, 1966.
Shadow of Wealth. Accra: Anowuo Educational Publications, 1966.
A Woman in her Prime. Heinemann, 1967.

Kurankyi-Taylor, Dorothy. *Reflected Thoughts.* Ilfracombe: Stockwell, 1959.

Mopeli-Paulus, A. S. *Blanket Boy.* New York: Crowell, 1953.
Turn to the Dark. Cape, 1956.

Munonye, John. *The Only Son.* Heinemann, 1966.

Namukwaya, Elvania. *Keeping Up With the Mukasas.* Performed at the Uganda Drama Festival, 1963. Mimeo.

Ngugi, James. *The Black Hermit.* Kampala: Uganda National Theatre, 1962.
A Grain of Wheat. Heinemann, 1967.
The River Between. Heinemann, 1965.
Weep Not Child. Heinemann, 1964.

Nicol, Abioseh. *The Truly Married Woman and Other Stories.* Oxford University Press, 1965.

Nicol, Abioseh. *Two African Tales: The Leopard Hunt and The Devil at Yelahun Bridge.* Cambridge: Cambridge University Press, 1965.

Njau, Rebecca. *The Scar.* Moshi: Kibo Art Gallery, 1965.

Nwankwo, Nkem. *Danda.* Andre Deutsch, 1964.

Eroya. Ibadan: Mbari, 1963. Mimeo.
Tales Out of School. Lagos: African Universities Press, 1964.
Nwanodi, Okogbule Glory. *Icheke and Other Poems*. Ibadan: Mbari, 1964.
Nwapa, Flora. *Efuru*. Heinemann, 1966.
Nzekwu, Onuora. *Blade Among the Boys*. Hutchinson, 1962.
Highlife for Lizards. Hutchinson, 1965.
Wand of Noble Wood. Hutchinson, 1961.
Nzekwu, Onuora and Crowder, Michael. *Eze Goes to School*. Lagos: African Universities Press, 1963.
Odeku, E. Latunde. *Twilight Out of the Night*. Ibadan: University of Ibadan Press, 1964.
Ogot, Grace. *The Promised Land*. Nairobi; East African Publishing House, 1966.
Ogunyemi, Wale. *Business Express*. Oshogbo: Theatre Express Sketches, 1966.
Okara, Gabriel. *The Voice*. Andre Deutsch, 1964.
Okigbo, Christopher. *Heaven's Gate*. Ibadan: Mbari, 1962.
Okigbo, Christopher. *Limits*. Ibadan: Mbari, 1964.
Okogie, M. O. *Songs of Africa*. Ilfracombe: Stockwell, 1961.
Olagoke, E. Olu. *The Incorruptible Judge*. Evans Brothers, 1962.
The Irokoman and the Wood Carver. Evans Brothers, 1963.
Osadebay, Dennis. *Africa Sings*. Ilfracombe: Stockwell, 1952.
Parkes, Francis Ernest Kobina. *Songs from the Wilderness*. University of London Press, 1965.
Peters, Lenrie. *Poems*. Ibadan: Mbari, 1964.
Satellites. Heinemann, 1967.
The Second Round. Heinemann, 1965.
Rubadiri, David. *No Bride Price*. Nairobi: East African Publishing House, 1967.
Samkange, Stanlake. *On Trial for My Country*. Heinemann, 1966.
Segun, Mabel. *My Father's Daughter*. Lagos: African Universities Press, 1965.
Selormey, Francis. *The Narrow Path*. Heinemann, 1966.
Sofola, Samuel Adeniyi. *When a Philosopher Falls in Love*. New York: Commet Press, 1956.
Sofowote, Segun. *Sailor Boy in Town*. Oshogbo: Theatre Express Sketches, 1966.
Soyinka, Wole. *Before the Blackout*. Performed at Ibadan, 1965.

Mimeo.

A Dance of the Forests. Oxford University Press, 1963.

Five Plays. Oxford University Press, 1965.

The Interpreters. Andre Deutsch, 1965.

Kongi's Harvest. Ibadan University Press, 1967.

The Lion and the Jewel. Oxford University Press, 1963.

Three Plays. Ibadan: Mbari, 1963.

The Road. Oxford University Press, 1965.

Tutuola, Amos. *Ajaiyi and his Inherited Poverty.* Faber, 1967.

The Brave African Huntress. Faber, 1958.

Feather Woman of the Jungle. Faber, 1962.

My Life in the Bush of Ghosts. Faber, 1954.

The Palm-Wine Drunkard and his Dead Palm-Wine Tapster in the Deads' Town. Faber, 1952.

Simbi and the Satyr of the Dark Jungle. Faber, 1956.

Uzodinma, E. C. C. *Brink of Dawn: Stories from Nigeria.* Ikeja: Longmans of Nigeria, 1966.

Our Dead Speak. Longmans, 1967.

Periodical Anthologies

Mphahlele, Ezekiel (ed.). 'New East African Writing', *East Africa Journal*, Special Issue (September 1966).

'New Sum of Poetry from the Negro World', *Présence Africaine*, xxix (1966) 57.

Ngugi, James (ed.). 'Special Issue on Creative Writing', *East Africa Journal* (January 1968).

Okola, Leonard (ed.). 'East African Creative Writing', *East Africa Journal*, Special Issue (September 1967).

Rubadiri, David (ed.). 'East African New Writing', *East Africa Journal*, Special Issue (January 1967).

Literary Periodicals

Abbia.

Africa Report.

Black Orpheus.

Bulletin of the Association for African Literature in English.

Journal of Commonwealth Literature.

New African.

Nigeria Magazine.

Okyeame.

Penpoint.
Présence Africaine.
Times Literary Supplement.
Transition.

SECONDARY SOURCES

General Books

Abraham, William E. *The Mind of Africa*. Chicago: University of Chicago Press, 1962.

Beier, Ulli (ed.). *Introduction to Africa Literature: An Anthology of Critical Writing on African and Afro-American Literature and Oral Tradition*. Evanston: Northwestern University Press, 1967.

Blotner, Joseph. *The Political Novel*. Garden City: Doubleday and Company, 1955.

Bown, Lalage and Crowder, Michael (ed.). *First International Congress of Africanists proceedings: Accra, December 11–18, 1962*. Evanston: Northwestern University Press, 1964.

Bowra, C. M. *Poetry and Politics, 1900–60*. Cambridge: Cambridge University Press, 1966.

Dewey, John. *Art as Experience*. New York: Capricorn Books, 1958.

Diop, Cheikh Anta. *The Cultural Unity of Negro Africa: The Domains of Patriarchy and Matriarchy in Classical Antiquity*. Paris: Présence Africaine, 1962.

Gleason, Judith Illsley. *This Africa: Novels by West Africans in English and French*. Evanston: Northwestern University Press, 1965.

Jahn, Janheinz. *Muntu: An Outline of the New African Culture*. Translated by Marjorie Arene. New York: Grove Press, 1961.

Lowenthal, Leo. *Literature and the Image of Man*. Boston: Beacon Press, 1957.

Marx, K. and Engels, F. *Literature and Art: Selections from their Writings*. New York: International Publishers, 1947.

Moore, Gerald. *Seven African Writers*. Oxford University Press, 1962.

(ed.). *African Literature and the Universities*. Kbadan: University of Ibadan Press, 1965.

Mphahlele, Ezekiel. *The African Image*. Faber and Faber, Ltd., 1962.

Nannes, Caspar H. *Politics in the American Drama*. Washington: Catholic University of America Press, 1960.

Nicol, Abioseh. *Africa: A Subjective View*. Cambridge, Mass.: Harvard University Press, 1964.

Orwell, George. *A Collection of Essays*. Garden City: Doubleday and Company, 1967.

Press, John (ed.). *Commonwealth Literature: Unity and Diversity in a Common Culture*. Heinemann, 1965.

Ramsaran, John A. *New Approaches to African Literature: A Guide to Negro-African Writing and Related Studies*. Ibadan: Ibadan University Press, 1965.

Ramsaran, John A. and Janheinz Jahn. *Approaches to African Literature: Non-English Writings by Janheinz Jahn and English Writing in West Africa by John Ramsaran*. Ibadan: Ibadan University Press, 1959.

Tucker, Martin. *Africa in Modern Literature: A Survey of Contemporary Writing in English*. New York: Frederick Ungar Publishing Company, 1967.

Wauthier, Claude. *The Literature and Thought of Modern Africa*. Translated by Shirley Kay. New York: Praeger, 1967.

Articles

Achebe, Chinua. 'The Black Writers Burden', *Présence Africaine*, English edition, xxxi No. 59 (1966) 135–40.

'The Novelist As Teacher', *New Statesman* (29 January 1965) pp. 161–2.

'The Role of the Writer in a New Nation', *Nigerian Libraries*, i No. 3 (September 1964) 113–19.

'The Role of the Writer in a New Nation', *Nigeria Magazine*, lxxxi (1964) 157–60.

'Africa on Record', *Times Literary Supplement* (11 June 1964) pp. 501–2.

Aig-Imoukhuede, M. 'On Being a West African Writer', *Ibadan*, xii (1961) 11–12.

'Are There Underdeveloped Writers?', *Times Literary Supplement*, xxvii (May 1965) 429–30.

Awooner-Williams, George. 'Fresh Vistas for African Literature', *African Review*, i 1 (May 1965) 35, 38.

Banham, Martin J. 'The Beginnings of a Nigerian Literature in English', *Review of English Literature*, III No. 2 (April 1962) 88–9.

Banham, Martin J. 'Drama in the Commonwealth: Nigeria', *New Theatre Magazine*, IV (July 1960) 18–21.

'Notes on Nigerian Theatre: 1966', *Bulletin of the Association for African Literature in English*, IV (1966) 31–66.

'A Piece We May Fairly Call Our Own', *Ibadan*, XII (June 1966) 15–18.

Banham, Martin J. and Ramsaran, John. 'West African Writing', *Books Abroad*, V No. 36 (Autumn 1962) 371–4.

Beier, Ulli. 'The Conflict of Cultures in West African Poetry', *Black Orpheus*, I (1957) 17–21.

'Contemporary African Poetry in English', *Makerere Journal*, XI No. 4 (1962) 11.

'Some Nigerian Poets', *Présence Africaine*, English edition, IV –V, Nos. 32–3 (1960) 50–63.

'Three Mbari Poets', *Black Orpheus*, XII (1963) 46–50.

Bilen, Max. 'The African Poet as Bard of His People', *Présence Africaine*, English edition, XXVI No. 54 (1965) 141–5.

p'Bitek, Okot. 'The Self in African Imagery', *Transition*, IV No. 15 (1964) 32.

Clark, John Pepper. 'Another Kind of Poetry', *Transition*, V No. 25 (1966) 17–22.

'Aspects of Nigerian Drama', *Nigeria Magazine*, LXXXIX (1966) 118–26.

'A Note on Nigerian Poetry', *Présence Africaine*, English edition, XXX No. 58 (1966) 55–64.

Clark, John Pepper. 'Poetry in Africa Today', *Transition*, IV No. 18 (1965) 20–6.

'Themes of African Poetry of English Expression', *Présence Africaine*, English edition, XXVI No. 54 (1965) 70–89.

Collins, H. R. 'Founding a New National Literature: The Ghost Novels of Amos Tutuola', *Critique*, IV (1960) 17–28.

Cook, David. 'Of the Strong Breed', *Transition*, III No. 13 (1964) 38–40.

Crowder, M. 'Tradition and Change in Nigerian Literature', *Bulletin of the Association for African Literature in English*, III (1965) 1–17.

Dathorne, O. R. 'The African Novel: A Document to Experiment', *Bulletin of the Association for African Literature in English,* III (1965) 18–39.

'Document and Imagination', *New African,* III (April 1966) 57–9.

'Pioneer African Drams: Heroines and the Church', *Bulletin of the Association for African Literature in English,* IV (1966) 19–23.

'Writing from Nigeria', *Bulletin of the Association for African Literature in English,* II, 31–2.

Davidson, Basil. 'African Literature Now', *West Africa,* MCLVI No. 27 (June 1964) 711.

DeGraft, J. C. 'Drama Workship, 1963', *Okyeame,* XI No. 1 (1964) 48–50.

Demott, Benjamin. 'An Unprofessional Eye. Oyiemu-O?' *American Scholar,* XXXII No. 2 (Spring 1963) 292–306.

Dei-Anang, M. F. 'A Writers Outlook', *Okyeame,* I (January 1961) 40–3.

Drayton, A. D. 'The Return of the Past in the Nigerian Novel', *Ibadan,* X (1960) 27–30.

Echeruo, J. C. 'Traditional and Borrowed Elements in Nigerian Poetry', *Nigeria Magazine,* LXXXIX (1966) 142–55.

Edwards, Paul. 'The Novel in West Africa', *Overseas Quarterly,* III (June 1963) 176–7.

Edwards, Paul and Carroll, David R. 'Approach to the Novel in West Africa', *Phylon,* XXIII No. 4 (Winter 1962) 319–31.

Ekwensi, Cyprian. 'African Literature', *Nigeria Magazine,* LXXXIII (1964) 294–9.

'The Literary Influences on a Young Nigerian', *Times Literary Supplement,* IV (June 1964) 475–6.

'Problems of Nigerian Writers', *Nigeria Magazine,* LXXVIII (1963) 217–19.

Esslin, Martin. 'Two African Playwrights', *Black Orpheus,* XIX (1966) 33–9.

Ferguson, John. 'Nigerian Poetry in English', *English,* XV, (Autumn 1965) 231–5.

Fischer, S. L. 'Africa: Mother and Muse', *Antioch Review,* XXI (Fall 1961) 305–18.

Gerard, Albert S. 'The Neo-African Novel', *Africa Report,* IX 7 (July 1964) 3–5.

Gleason, J. 'Out of the Irony of Words', *Transition*, IV No. 18 (1965) 34–8.

Hanshell, Deryck. 'African Writing Today', *Month*, XXXII (November 1964) 246–54.

Hopkinson, Tom. 'Deaths and Entrances: The Emergence of African Writing', *Twentieth Century*, CLXV No. 986 (April 1959) 332–42.

Jaffe, H. 'African Literary Studies', *New African*, V 9 (1963) 13–14.

Jones, D. A. N. 'Jombo', *New Statesman*, XXIX (January 1965) 164.

Jones, Eldred. 'Jungle Drums and Wailing Piano: West African Fiction and Poetry in English', *African Forum*, I No. 4 (Spring 1966) 93–106.

July, Robert W. 'African Literature and the African Personality', *Black Orpheus*, XIV (1964) 33–45.

Kennard, Peter. 'Recent African Dramas', *Bulletin of the Association for African Literature in English*, II (n.d.) 11–18.

Khan, Ras. 'The Poetry of Dr. R. E. G. Armattoe', *Présence Africaine*, XII (1957) 32–6.

Killam, Douglas. 'Recent African Fiction', *Bulletin of the Association for African Literature in English*, II (n.d.) 1–10.

Kolade, Christopher. 'Looking at Drama in Nigeria', *African Forum*, I No. 3 (Winter 1966) 77–9.

Lagneau-Kesteloot, L. 'Problems of the Literary Critic in Africa', *Abbia*, VIII (1965) 29–44.

Lindfors, Bernth. 'Five Nigerian Novels', *Books Abroad*, IV (Autumn 1965) 411–13.

'Literature as Symptom', *Times Literary Supplement*, 11 (January 1963) 25.

'The Literary Drought', *East African Journal*, XI 10 (March 1966) 11–15.

Lo Liyong, Taban. 'Can We Correct Literary Barrenness in East Africa?' *East Africa Journal* (December 1966) pp. 5–13.

Maclean, U. 'Wole Soyinka', *Black Orpheus*, XV (1964) 46–51.

Matthew, Geruasse. 'The Literature of Africa', *New Blackfriars*, XLVI (October 1964) 41–3.

McHardy, Cecile. 'The Performing Arts in Ghana', *African Forum*, I No. 1 (Summer 1965) 113–17.

Mezu, S. Okechukwu. 'The Origins of African Poetry', *Journal of the New African Literature and the Arts*, ii (Fall 1966) 66–123.

Moore, Gerald. 'African Literature Seen from Salisbury', *Présence Africaine*, English edition, cxi No. 31 (1960) 87–94.

'English Words, African Lives', *Présence Africaine*, English edition, xxvi No. 54 (1965) 90–101.

'Time and Experience in African Poetry', *Transition*, vi No. 26 (1966) 18–22.

Moore, Gerald and Stuart, Donald. 'African Literature, French and English', *Makerere Journal*, viii (1963) 29–34.

Mphahlele, Ezekiel. 'African Literature for Beginners', *Africa Today*, xiv No. 1 (January 1967) 25–31.

'The Language of African Literature', *Harvard Educational Review*, xxxiv No. 2 (Spring 1964) 298–306.

'Writers in Search of Themes', *West African Review*, xxxii No. 416 (August 1964) 40–1.

'Nation to Nation', *Times Literary Supplement*, xv (March 1963) 177.

Nazareth, Peter. 'The African Writer and Commitment', *Transition*, iv No. 19 (1965) 6–7.

Nicol, Abioseh. 'Negritude in West Africa', *New Statesman*, x (September 1960) 353–4.

'The Soft Pink Palms', *Présence Africaine*, English edition, viii –x (1956) 107–21.

'West African Poetry', *Africa South in Exile*, v No. 3 (1961) 18–21.

Nkosi, Lewis. 'African Fiction: South Africa Protest', *Africa Report*, vii No. 9 (October 1962) 3–6.

'African Literature: English Speaking West Africa', *Africa Report*, vii No. 11 (December 1962) 15–17.

'Against the Tribe', *New African*, iv No. 3 (May 1965) 70–1.

'Some Conversations with African Writers', *Africa Report*, ix No. 7 (July 1964) 7–21.

'Where Does African Literature Go From Here?' *Africa Today*, xi No. 9 (December 1966) 7–11.

Macauley, R. 'African Literature: First Generation', *New Republic*, cxlvi (23 April 1962) 32–5.

Obumselu, Ben. 'The Background of Modern African Literature', *Ibadan*, xxii (June 1966) 46–59.

Ogunba, Oyin. 'Theatre in Nigeria', *Présence Africaine*, English edition, xxx No. 58 (1966) 63–8.

Okara, Gabriel. 'African Speech–English Words', *Transition*, III No. 10 (1963) 15–16.

Parry, J. 'Nigerian Novelists', *Contemporary Review*, cc (1961) 377–81.

Povey, John F. 'Changing Themes in the Nigerian Novel', *Journal of the New African Literature*, I (Spring 1966) 3–11.

'Contemporary West African Writing in English', *Books Abroad*, XL No. 3 (Summer 1966) 253–60.

'Wole Soyinka and the Nigerian Drama', *Tri-Quarterly*, II (Spring 1966) 20.

Recrod, Barry. 'Notes on Two Nigerian Playwrights', *New African*, IV No. 7 (September 1965) 171.

Reed, John. 'Between Two Worlds: Some Notes on the Presentation by African Novelists of the Individual in Modern African Society', *Makerere Journal*, VII (1963) 1–14.

Redding, Saunders. 'Modern African Literature', *College Language Association Journal*, VII (March 1964).

Rubadiri, David. 'Why African Literature?', *Transition*, IV No. 15 (1964) 39–42.

Shelton, Austin J. 'Ewo!', *Transition*, IV No. 20 (1965) 7–9.

'Behaviour and Cultural Value in West African Stories: Literary Sources for the Study of Cultural Contact', *Africa*, XXXIV (1964) 353–9.

'Pan Africanism and Beautiful Feathers', *Books Abroad*, XXXIX (1965) 34–6.

'Some Problems of Intercommunication', *Journal of Modern African Studies*, XI 3 (1964) 395–403.

Shore, Herbert. 'Drums, Dances and then Some', *Texas Quarterly*, VII 2 (Summer 1964) 225–31.

Sieber, Roy. 'Masks as Agents of Social Control', *African Studies Bulletin*, V No. 5 (1962) 62.

Society of Nigerian Authors. 'The Headline Novels of Africa', *West Africa*, XXVIII No. 2360 (August 1962) 941.

'Something New Out of Africa', *Times Literary Supplement*, VI (March 1959) 131.

Soyinka, Wole. 'From a Common Back Cloth; A Reassessment of the African Literary Image', *American Scholar*, XXXII (Summer 1963) 387–96.

'The Writer in an African State', *Transition*, vi 31 (1967) 11–13.

Sterling, Thomas. 'Africa's Black Writers', *Holiday*, xvi No. 2 (February 1967) 131–40.

Tolson, Melvin. 'Three African Poets', *African Forum*, i No. 3 (Winter 1966) 121–3.

Treadgold, Mary. 'Writers in Search of Themes', *West African Review*, xxxii No. 413 (May 1962) 57–61.

Tucker, Martin. 'The Headline Novels of Africa', *West Africa*, No. 2356 (July 1962) p. 829.

'Three West African Novels', *Africa Today*, xii No. 9 (November 1965) 10–14.

'West African Literature: The Second Decade', *Africa Today*, xiii No. 5 (May 1966) 7–9; dciii No. 6 (June 1966) 7–8.

Wake, Clive. 'African Literary Criticism', *Comparative Literature Studies*, i No. 3 (1964) 197–205.

Wali, Obiajunwa. 'The Dead End of African Literature', *Transition*, cxi 10 (1963).

'The Individual and the Novel in Africa', *Transition*, iv No. 18 (1965) 31–3.

Whiteley, Wilfred H. 'The Concept of an African Prose Literature', *Diogenes*, xxxvii (Spring 1962) 24–49.

'Who Reads It?', *Times Literary Supplement*, xvi (November 1965) 801.

'Writing in West Africa. A Chance to Adapt and Experiment', *Times Literary Supplement*, x (August 1962) 570–1.

Unpublished Manuscripts

Bahou, Victor. 'Political Drama in America Since 1930.' Unpublished Ph.D. dissertation, Syracuse University, 1965.

McDowell, Robert Eugene. 'Africa-English Novel.' Unpublished Ph.D. dissertation, University of Denver, 1966.

Moore, J. A. 'Social Strain and Cultural Conflict in West African Novels.' Unpublished Ph.D. dissertation, Boston University, 1966.

Kozak, Yitka R. 'The Reflection in Czech Literature of Political Changes in Eastern Europe, 1948–1965.' Unpublished Ph.D. dissertation, Syracuse University, 1967.

Ruberti, Ernest N. 'Social and Political Thought in the

Modern Indian Novel (in English).' Unpublished Master's thesis, Syracuse University, 1966.

Spann, P. A. 'African Literature, History and Criticism: Descriptive Survey of Creative African Literature and the Social Forces Influencing It.' Unpublished Master's thesis, University of Chicago, 1965.

Stanislaus, J. 'The Growth of African Literature: A Survey of the Works Published by African Writers in English and French.' Unpublished Ph.D. dissertation, University of Montreal, 1952.

Index

Abbs, A.
  Ashanti Boy 117
Abruquah, J. W. 103
  The Catechist 126
Achebe, C. 10–11, 31, 50, 96, 124, 130
  Arrow of God 86, 125
  A Man of the People 19, 27, 36, 41, 43, 45,
    63
  No Longer at Ease 21, 36, 76, 84, 88, 107
  Things Fall Apart 61, 86
Agunwa, C.
  More Than Once 76
Aluko, T. M.
  Kinsman and Foreman 33
  One Man, One Matchet 31, 33–4, 85
  One Man, One Wife 33
Armattoe, R. E. G. 97
  'Servant–Kings' 47
  'They Said' 47
Awoonor-Williams, G. 22, 49, 99
  'Consummation' 115
  'Exiles' 81

Beier, U. 17
p'Bitek, O. 56–7
  Song of Lawino 44, 53
Blotner, J.
  The Political Novel 3–4
Brew, K.
  'The Search' 98

Clark, J. P. 112
Conton, W. 20–1, 119–20, 126

Dei-Anang, M. 10, 100
  'Africa Speaks' 108
  'Whither Bound Africa' 112
Duodu, C.
  The Gab Boys 80

Easmon, R. S.
  Dear Parent and Ogre 119
  The New Patriots 36, 40–1

Egbuna, O. B.
  Wind Versus Polygamy 40, 64
Ekwensi, C. 118
  Beautiful Feathers 49, 75–6, 84, 108
  Iska 36, 59
  Jagua Nana 20, 40, 76, 130
  When Love Whispers 26, 76, 88
Ekwere, J. 110
  'Rejoinder' 12

Gathern, M. 10

Henshaw, J. 73
  Medicine for Love 43

Ike, V. Chikwuemeka
  Toads for Supper 28

Jones-Quartey, K. A. B.
  'Stranger, Why Do You Wonder So'
    111

Kachingwe, A.
  No Easy Task 49, 63, 130–1
Kayira, L.
  The Looming Shadow 88
Kihohia, S. 96
Kimenye, B. 62
Konadu, A.
  Shadow of Wealth 59

Lowenthal, L. 4

Matiro, W. 87
Mensah, A. K. 111
Mopeli-Paulus, A. 85
  Blanket Boy 128
Munonye, J.
  The Only Son 58, 126

Ngugi, J. 61, 102–3, 131
  A Grain of Wheat 43, 49, 107, 129
  Weep Not Child 74, 127, 129

Nicol, A.
  The Truly Married Woman 11, 60
  Two African Tales 11
Nwanodi, O. G. 23
Nwanko, N.
  Danda 87
Nwapa, F. 57
  Efuru 58
Nwosu, T. C.
  'B. B.' 29
Nzekwu, O.
  Blade Among the Boys 91
  Highlife for Lizards 67, 127
  Wand of Noble Wood 84

Ogot, G. 60, 62
  The Promised Land 61, 86, 118
Okara, G.
  The Voice 28, 62, 118
Orwell, George 4
Osadebay, D. C. 105
  'Young Africa's Lament' 104
  'Young Africa's Plea' 104

Parkes, F. E. K. 97, 109
  'Two Deaths, One Grave' 106

Peters, L.
  'In the Beginning' 108
Poore, C. 4

Rubadiri, D. 51
  No Bride Price 35, 37, 74, 76
  Stanley Meets Mutesa 97

Samkange, S.
  On Trial for my Country 99
Segun, M. 12
  'Second Olympus' 101
Shelton, A. J. 9, 84
Sieber, R. 9
Soyinka, W. 28, 62, 91
  A Dance of the Forest 61
  The Interpreters 22, 25, 31, 41, 51, 59, 76, 81, 85, 88
  Kongi's Harvest 47, 62
  The Lion and the Jewel 26, 84
  The Road 130
  The Strong Breed 76
  The Swamp Dwellers 79

Wake, C. H. 5

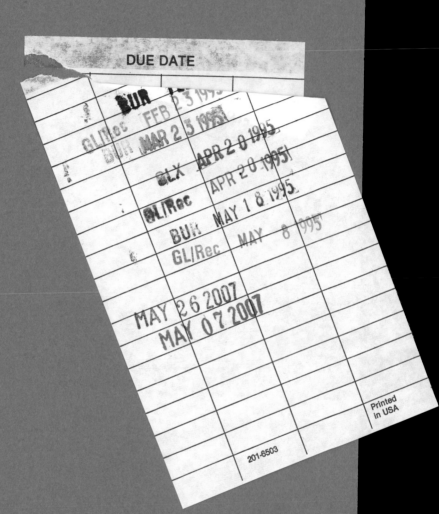